Missions at the Crossroads

Missions at the Crossroads

THE INDIGENOUS CHURCH—
A SOLUTION FOR THE UNFINISHED TASK

by

T. Stanley Soltau, D.D.

Author of

Who Do Men Say That I Am?

BAKER BOOK HOUSE
Grand Rapids 6, Michigan
1955

Library of Congress Catalog Card Number: 55-12157

PHOTOLITHOPRINTED BY CUSHING - MALLOY, INC.
ANN ARBOR, MICHIGAN, UNITED STATES OF AMERICA
1955

15010

FOREWORD

Missions are at the crossroads, and here is a book that points the direction to take. It will come as somewhat of a surprise to many Christians to understand that most missions are now realizing that many of the methods hitherto employed by them are no longer recognized as effective. Sufficient time has passed since the beginning of the so-called "modern missions period" to evaluate with conclusiveness the effectiveness of the prevailing methods which have been followed. Christian missions generally are reaching the conclusion that there must be a basic change from the old-line methods to what is now popularly referred to as the method of "the indigenous church."

Christian missions will never be at the crossroads as far as its message is concerned. The gospel will ever be "the power of God unto salvation to everyone that believeth." This is the gospel that must be preached to every creature. Missions today are at the crossroads that will doubtless determine the final form of its method of completing the task of world evangelization.

"The indigenous church—a solution for the unfinished task" is no mere sub-title. These words crystallize a vision and a method. Will the task ever be finished? With utter certainty the Word of God answers that it will. The only miracle recorded in each of the four Gospels, the feeding of the five thousand, answers that it will be finished by a miracle. Just as the Lord Jesus worked a miracle at the hands of His disciples which resulted in feeding that multitude with bread, even so today He is working a mightier miracle at the hands of His Church which will result in carrying to the uttermost part of the earth the "living Bread come down from God out of Heaven." The world is going to be evangelized by the miracle of the risen Son of God who said "I will build My Church." *Only within the framework of the indigenous church policy can liberty be found for the full expression and outworking of that mighty power.*

Anticipating this present movement for an indigenous church —establishing from their very beginning self-supporting, self-governing, and self-propagating churches—the American Presbyterian Mission in Korea inaugurated and carried out for two generations these New Testament principles. The result of the application of these principles in Korea has been termed "the miracle of modern missions." The mission work in Korea has become a pattern now widely followed by missions in other lands.

For twenty-five years Dr. T. Stanley Soltau was one of the leaders in the Korean mission, directing pastoral, evangelistic, and educational work. When the crisis developed in the history of Korean missions, caused by the imperial order commanding Christians to worship at the Shinto shrines, Dr. Soltau was one of the missionaries who stood firmly against any such compromise with idolatry.

With a background of these twenty-five years of experience spent at the heart of this unique missionary movement, Dr. Soltau is qualified as few others could be to set forth the principles of the indigenous church, illustrating them from his own actual experience in Korea. This book abounds in such illustrations. The author is not arguing for a theory; he is demonstrating the effectiveness of missionary methods clearly revealed in the New Testament and wrought out through the experience of the Korean mission.

The establishment of an indigenous church is not without serious problems. These problems are faced in a frank and wise way, and the solution is suggested by one who has found that when these problems were met in his own experience there was an answer. The growth of nationalism, the new attitude of Orientals toward Westerners, the new economic and political situation, and the rise of Communism, as well as the internal problems connected with the development of an indigenous church, are given special consideration.

Dr. Soltau's book should be of special value to mission classes in seminaries, Bible colleges, and Bible institutes, but of no less value to every Christian who desires to be better informed regarding what may well be the last great development in missionary history until its consummation at the glorious appearing of Jesus Christ.

G. ALLEN FLEECE
President, Columbia Bible College
Columbia, South Carolina

PREFACE

Missions at the Crossroads! Yes, they are at the crossroads and the question as to what the future holds for Christian missions is one which concerns every intelligent believer today. From almost every country come disquieting reports. In China the Communists have rapidly engulfed the whole of that mighty empire. Oppression and curtailment of liberty have come in like a flood and all mission work has been brought to a complete standstill. The North of Korea is completely in the hands of Communists and all of Southeast Asia is feeling the impact of the tremendous surge. India, having secured its independence from the British Raj, and divided into Hindustan and Pakistan, is facing a world of complex problems, and as yet no one can speak with assurance of the final outcome, particularly as it affects the foreign missionary.

From Africa word has been received that with the upsurge of nationalism and the influence of Communism, it is likely that within another ten years foreign missionary work in that vast continent may be brought to a close. In Latin America also the same forces of opposition are at work; the securing of visas for missionaries is becoming increasingly difficult and restrictions on the activities of those who are already there are likely to be intensified. Behind the Iron Curtain in Europe no Christian missionaries are allowed and similar prohibitions have come from behind the "Bamboo Curtain" in Asia.

What then is to be the future of the Christian movement in these territories already cut off and what is to be done in those lands over which the Red menace is already hanging like a dark cloud, threatening to sweep away all foreign influences and interests, especially those which are there to proclaim the gospel of Jesus Christ? Should young missionaries be encouraged to go out in the face of all this uncertainty? How should we pray for those who have already gone? Should the uncertainty of the future affect the work and the policies of those now on the fields, and what can be done to prepare for the crisis, the approach of which is so rapid? All of these and many similar questions are constantly in the minds of students of missions, and are pressing for an immediate answer.

Of one thing we can be certain—though the foreign missionaries may be forced to leave their fields, the national Christians cannot, and must remain. Whatever political changes may

7

take place, the Christian constituency will be there. Upon the national Christian leaders, therefore, must fall the heavy responsibility of directing the work and making the decisions upon which the whole future of the Christian movement in those lands will depend. The church will doubtless be subjected to heavy pressure, if not to cruel persecution. It may be forced to go underground, as was the case in the early centuries of the Roman Empire, and as it has had to do in Communist Russia. From past history and from more recent experiences, however, we believe that come what may, God, who is still on His Throne, will continue to vindicate the faith of His servants who put their trust in Him and refuse to give up their faith in the Lord Jesus Christ.

The responsibility of all who are engaged in foreign missionary work in the light of these conditions is clear. Every effort possible should be made to carry on regardless of uncertainty and of the difficulty of conditions until the doors are actually closed. No retreat before then can be contemplated. But that is not all—special steps should be taken in every possible way while the doors remain open to strengthen the national churches already established, by placing in the hands of those churches and their leaders full responsibility for the threefold task of self-propagation, self-government and self-support. Moreover, mission policies and methods should be adopted so that whatever stage of development has been reached, and even in the new groups and churches which are now being brought into existence, all of them from now on should be placed on a self-contained and self-sustaining basis and thus become truly indigenous. Such policies have already been in operation in certain fields, notably Korea, where the church has from the beginning been thus established.

During the recent World War national Christians in Ethiopia, without foreign missionaries; in China, occupied by the Japanese forces; in Korea, overrun by Communist influence, have shown the remarkable way in which God raises up His leaders. They not only carried on the work, but pressed forward with even greater diligence, under conditions of extreme difficulty, and in many cases with far greater success than when foreign missionaries had been in almost complete control. In this book a general outline of these policies is set forth to show the Scriptural basis for carrying on work in this way, and also to give illustrations of what has been accomplished where such methods have been given a fair trial. With conditions as they are today missionaries and prospective missionaries should think through the whole question again prayerfully and objectively. This should be done so that God may first call forth a new spirit of discernment and of courageous faith and then use it for a new manifestation of His omnipotent power in the gospel of our Lord Jesus Christ.

The little village of Sorai on the West Coast of Korea has interesting connections with the entrance of the gospel into that country. During the first half of the 19th century Portuguese Roman Catholic priests from China were secretly landed from fishing boats on small islands just off the coast and were smuggled ashore by night so that Sorai became a gateway for the entrance of Christianity in those early years. Later, however, it became of even greater significance in connection with the beginning of Protestant missions. A young merchant from that village went up to Manchuria on business and while there fell seriously ill. In the providence of God he entered a hospital conducted by the Scotch Presbyterian Mission and after several weeks of treatment was restored to health. On his recovery he asked the physicians what he could do to show his appreciation and was told that since it was through the mercy of the Lord that his body had been healed, he should accept His Son Christ Jesus as Saviour for the healing of his soul. The young Korean did so and on his return to Korea hid in his pack some New Testaments and Christian books. It was at considerable risk that he did this, for Christianity was under the Imperial ban in Korea, following the great persecution of the Roman Catholic Christians in 1864, in which not less than 10,000 were martyred, including a number of Portuguese priests.

On his arrival at his home in Sorai, Mr. Song told his family and friends of his new-found faith, reading to them from his New Testament and explaining the meaning of the gospel. When in 1885 news reached Sorai of the arrival of some missionaries in Seoul, a letter was sent to the capital inviting them to visit the village of Sorai. Dr. Horace Underwood, in reply, made the week's trip by pony, and examined and baptized those of the new believers who proved their readiness to make public profession of their faith.

Years passed and in the summer of 1931 the 45th anniversary

of the erection of the first church building at Sorai was observed
with fitting ceremonies. Pastor Song, the younger brother of
the man who had brought the news of the gospel from Manchuria, and one of the first ordained ministers of the Korean
Presbyterian Church, was present from Shanghai for the occasion. To a large crowd of interested Korean Christians and
missionaries gathered on the church property, he told of the
experiences of the early days. Not long after Dr. Underwood's
first visit the little group of Christians, in the joy of their new-
found faith, began telling the news to their friends. The vener-
able Pastor Song, looking the part of a real patriarch, with long
white beard and flowing white Korean robe, reported: "Before
long the interest of the village in animal sacrifices to the guardian
spirits of the village waned and in a year or two only one man,
with the sacrifice of one chicken, observed the age-old ceremonies." Turning to his congregation, Pastor Song added, "Soon
after this the sacrificial site came into the hands of the Christians and you today are sitting in the shade of this grove of
trees in which for hundreds of years the goats, pigs, and chickens
sacrificed to the spirits had been tied. The building on your
left was our first church building and was also the first Christian church to be erected by Korean Christians unaided, in the
entire country. Today we are celebrating the 45th anniversary
of our old building and the opening of our new church, which
seats between three and four hundred people." During that
same length of time the Presbyterian Church of Korea had been
established with some twenty presbyteries and its own General
Assembly. Over 100,000 baptized members were on its rolls,
and in addition to maintaining the entire expense of the hundreds of churches scattered throughout the country, for over
twenty years their Board of Foreign Missions had supported
three ordained Korean pastors as foreign missionaries in China
and the Board of Home Missions was maintaining a force which
had grown to over twenty workers in the Island of Quelpart,
off the southern tip of Korea, and among the Koreans in Japan,
Manchuria, and Shanghai.

Korea has been one of the most fruitful of all mission fields
and while there have been several factors in the amazingly rapid
growth of the church there, the most important has been that
of the methods and policies which have been used, whereby
from the very beginning the responsibility for maintenance and
leadership has been with the church. At that time the plan

seemed almost revolutionary in comparison with the usual mission methods, but this indigenous church policy has been tried in other mission fields also, with marked success; and more and more forward-looking missionaries are coming to realize that this method of planting a church is not only in accord with the early Apostolic methods but is the only one which will insure rapid and sturdy growth. To make plain its salient features is the purpose of this book. Too often the idea of establishing or building a church has been emphasized with the thought uppermost that the missionary, like a builder, must lay in place each stone until the work is nearly complete. In reality, the missionary has the responsibility for only part of the seed-sowing and then the cultivation of the young plants, but the church itself grows by the power of the Holy Spirit. It requires therefore in a sense to be left to itself that it may grow by itself, for only then can it rapidly become sturdy and vigorous.

CONTENTS

Contents

CHAPTER I

INTRODUCTORY—

THE PURPOSE OF CHRISTIAN MISSIONS

A N OUTSTANDING feature in the phenomenal development and advance of modern industry has been its careful analysis of these three factors of any prospective new enterprise: (1) its need, (2) the essential features of the product best
suited to meet that need, and (3) the most effective method of
obtaining or manufacturing the required product.

The same basic and thorough analysis should be applied
to the planning for Christian work, so that waste effort, inex-
cusable bungling, and many trial-and-error forms of activity will
be avoided. This is especially true of mission work, wherein so
often the precedents set by pioneer workers have been followed
more or less blindly by their successors, without evaluating their
use for existing conditions.

The history of foreign missions has often been regarded
as containing some of the most glorious pages in the history
of the Christian church. When judged from the viewpoint of
heroism and consecration of the valiant men and women who
have gladly obeyed the call of their Master and have gone out
to live in the midst of conditions of extreme hardship and
danger, and when necessary, to die, that verdict is absolutely
true. With very limited material equipment they went out to
face insuperable obstacles. They mastered difficult and hitherto
unknown languages; they broke down the barriers of national
suspicion and ill-will. They overcame the bitter opposition of
centuries—old and well-entrenched systems of religion and
superstition in which peoples were enslaved. They braved the
danger of hostile pagans, of unsanitary and unhealthy living
conditions, preaching the everlasting gospel of the Lord Jesus
Christ by their lips and their lives in such a way that hard hearts
were touched, lives were transformed and in some cases, whole
nations were changed.

When the history of foreign missions is judged however
from the viewpoint of well-planned, efficient activity, the same

unequivocal, affirmative answer cannot always be given. In some mission fields, after generations of work, the churches are still far from strong and there has been disappointingly little to show for the arduous and painstaking efforts of the missionaries. Some of this, especially in Mohammedan lands, must be regarded as largely due to the strangle hold which Islam has had on the peoples. New conditions however have arisen in many lands as the result of the Second World War, which make this a peculiarly appropriate time for all interested in mission work to think through the basic problems. They should seek to analyze them along the three lines mentioned at the beginning of this chapter. It is also always helpful and sometimes startling to inquire how these problems were met by the Apostolic church under the leadership of the Holy Spirit. We shall try briefly to present some of the problems together with the answers found in the New Testament, and those which experiences in Korea and in other mission fields have given.

A Standard Definition of Missions

One of the classic definitions of the aim of missions is, "The proclamation of the gospel to the unconverted everywhere, according to the command of Christ." This definition, however, omits one of the most vital parts of the responsibility of missions. In Matthew 28:19-20 are the words of "The Great Commission." In the American Revised Version it reads: "Go ye therefore, and make disciples of all the nations, baptizing them into the name of the Father, and of the Son and of the Holy Spirit, teaching them to observe all things whatsoever I commanded you; and lo, I am with you always, even unto the end of the world." In this passage there are three important directives.

(1) "Make disciples"—The word "disciples" has largely dropped out of our vocabularies but in the Orient is still very common. It speaks of those who are the followers of a religious teacher, and who enjoy a peculiarly intimate relationship with him, sharing the same experiences and very often wearing a distinctive mark or badge showing to whom they belong. Very often the disciples of any given teacher will take on some of his mannerisms or characteristic ways of speech or conduct and to that extent become imitators of him. A true follower of the Lord Jesus Christ should enjoy this peculiarly intimate relationship of a disciple with his Master and be conscious of the fact that he is sharing experiences with his Lord and in his daily

conduct should manifest a distinction which lets the world know he belongs to Him.

(2) "Baptizing"—Baptism was the public ceremony by which a public profession of faith was made and signified admission into the organized body of believers. The rite of baptism has been so regarded and so practiced ever since, all down through the Christian era.

(3) "Teaching them to observe all things whatsoever I commanded you"—This indicates a definite body of truth or doctrine, the knowledge of which together with its application to daily living is essential for a life that is well-pleasing to God. The church today has very largely forgotten its responsibilities in this important matter of systematic indoctrination of its members and the application of those doctrines to daily living. From the example of the early church it is evident that the responsibility of witnessing rested upon each individual member of the church. All were regarded as witnesses and all were exhorted to "desire earnestly spiritual gifts" (I Cor. 14:1; 12:27-31), that their lives might bear the fruit of the Spirit and that they might become "epistles of Christ" (II Cor. 3:3), known and read of all men to the glory and praise of God.

Each convert in a new place should be regarded as the potential nucleus for a new group of believers and a new church. His home should become a Christian center of witnessing, to which others are attracted and thus won to faith in Christ. New birth means new life, and new life must develop and in turn be used by the Holy Spirit to beget new life in others.

The duty of "teaching them to observe all things whatsoever I command you" will concentrate on laying before each believer his responsibility to grow in grace, through a study and appreciation of God's Word and then a daily application of its truths to his life and associations, so that the life of Christ may become a dynamic, making him a living witness to others.

A Needed Clause Added

The definition which we have been discussing is deficient, in that it fails to put the proper emphasis upon the planting and establishing of an independent church. It not only overlooks this most important matter but it completely fails to mention either the establishment of a church as the goal of missions, or the additional qualifications that this church must be indigenous. In order to make this definition effective, an additional clause is needed to make it read as follows: "The aim of Christian missions is the proclaiming of the gospel to the unconverted everywhere, according to the command of Christ, with a view to the establishing of an indigenous church."

The work of missions has come to be regarded as that into which money must constantly be poured, and for which therefore appeals must be continually made. The result is that the criticism is often heard, "We have been sending out missionaries and money all these years and there is so little to show for it. I should think that the people out there should be beginning to pay their own expenses and carry on their own work by this time." This fact is true. We have every reason to expect that when results are permanent that the native churches should not only be self-sustaining, but ready also to adopt an aggressive policy for reaching others.

In a good many mission fields work has been begun with the general goal of preaching the gospel in order to save people from the thraldom of their sins and to bring into existence a new church or churches. It has been only after converts have been won that the many problems connected with the establishment, development, and the training of leadership of those churches has been considered. It has often resulted in great loss of time, much heartache for the missionaries, a painful revaluation of the methods used, and in some cases, an entirely new policy brought into being.

The experience of the work in Korea has shown that when, from the initial stages, the planting of an indigenous church is made the goal, and that every step is planned with that in view, it is possible to make two stages unnecessary. From the beginning the church can be indigenous. During the first few years its progress may seem to be a little slow, but after it has taken root, its rapidity of development will be a continual source of amazement and delight to all who have a part in it.

In the light of this definition of Christian missions, as amended, it will at once be apparent that in the estimate of its success, the answer will depend not upon the number of converts, but upon the degree to which that particular church or piece of work has become indigenous—able to carry on independently of support and leadership from outside sources. All new work should be initiated and all new problems met with this definite aim in mind.

It is highly important that missionary candidates be well

acquainted with the goal of mission work in terms of an indigenous church and with the New Testament principles by which this goal can be attained. To those going to mission fields where such methods have not been adopted an additional word of caution should be given in regard to difficulties to be met.

QUESTIONS FOR DISCUSSION

1. What three important matters need to be analyzed in the work of missions in common with modern industry? Write out your analysis of each one as applied to the work of missionaries.
2. Discuss the meaning of three "key" directives in the "Great Commission," particularly in their relation to missionary activity.
3. Discuss the bearing of these three commands on the activities of the church at home today and point out wherein it has failed.
4. What is the "additional clause" added to the standard definition of missions and what bearing should it have in the training of prospective missionaries to carry on this work?
5. In what way does omission of this clause make for confusion in the work of missions?

Chapter II

THE INDIGENOUS CHURCH

IN order to gain an adequate conception of the goal of all mission work, we should ask ourselves the question, What is meant by an indigenous church?

Definition of an Indigenous Church

Webster's Dictionary defines *indigenous* as "produced, growing, or living naturally in a country or climate; native." A church therefore is not indigenous until it becomes native to the country and grows there naturally, as part and parcel of the people among whom it has been planted. In common usage, an indigenous church is defined as a church that is *self-governing, self-supporting* and *self-propagating.* A brief discussion of this threefold description will be helpful. It is well to remember that a church is an organism and not an organ. That is to say, it is not built but grows of itself. Unless the life of the Lord Jesus Christ Himself indwells its members, it becomes a mechanical and spiritually lifeless organization.

The three marks of an indigenous church mentioned above are not the essential ingredients making the church indigenous so much as they are the results of the life within it. They become the means by which that divine life of the Son of God manifests itself in and through the lives of the members. Only as the church is under the domination of its Head (Eph. 1:22) and shows in some measure His fullness (Eph. 1:23), can it grow and be built up into Him (Eph. 4:15,16). It is easy to be so concerned with the outward organization that the inward life suffers from lack of care or emphasis. The growth of the inner life must be the first and greatest concern of all who desire to establish a church. If this is maintained as the chief interest, each church can (and should) be an indigenous unit from the beginning. A study of the methods used by the apostles, as recorded in the New Testament, reveals that they had clearly-defined principles for establishing an indigenous church.

Self-Government

Importance of Church Organization. The importance of

church organization is often not appreciated until a person is actually on the mission field and meets problems as they actually are. Even in this country, church organization and ecclesiastical machinery are not understood by many church members. In most mission fields where people have had little training in organizing a church, what methods to use, and how best to proceed, those problems take on supreme importance. Unless plans are thought through in advance, confusion and difficulties almost inevitably result. The ideal would be that every missionary going to the field should have in mind the kind of church to be organized, the methods of self-government to be employed and the best policy to be carried out. In the work of foreign missions as a whole, there have been two widely differing tendencies, both of which need to be guarded against.

The first of these tendencies is seen in the very natural desire of those sent out by denominational agencies to establish a church that is an exact replica of the one back home which has sent them forth as its representatives. Unfortunately, however, the fact that a particular form of organization has been successful in America, does not guarantee that it will be equally successful in Africa, India, or South America. Because of this misdirected purpose, in several fields the work has been dangerously over-organized; so that the machinery of over-organization has become burdensome to the infant church.

On the other hand, among inter-denominational missions, often referred to as "faith missions," there has been a tendency to go to the opposite extreme. With an expressed determination to be interested chiefly in the proclamation of the gospel, and with workers from various denominational backgrounds, there has been a danger of under-estimating the necessity and value of church organization. Frequently work has been begun without a carefully thought-out policy. As a result, while there may have been a larger number of converts won than in the case of better organized work, this tendency has shown a noticeable lack of progress in establishing churches able to carry on by themselves without the close supervision of a foreign missionary.

Along with this particular emphasis on the work of evangelism, there has been a failure to recognize the need of educational work for the training of future church leaders. Often prospective workers have been sent to institutions established by other missions, where work is carried on under different policies. As a result, confusion and difficulties of various kinds have arisen.

In order to avoid this and to have all leaders (foreign and national) working in harmony, it is essential that a uniform policy on church organization, together with an adequate plan for leadership training, be adopted and carried out. Next to systematic Bible instruction, there is nothing more important than the foregoing policy for retaining morale and solidarity among Christians, or for strengthening them in their stand against the impacts of heathenism and persecution.

Purpose of Church Organization. In order that the church may assume the entire responsibility for deciding upon and carrying out its policy on various questions, there must be organization. Among these the most important factors are:

(1) Standards of admission to membership.
(2) Standards of Christian living (Acts 15:19,20).
(3) Instruction and discipline of members.
(4) Methods of church propagation.
(5) The form and the administration of organization and government.
(6) Doctrinal standards.

The above list of responsibilities is written in what might be regarded as the ascending scale of importance, and they will therefore probably be taken over by the infant church in that same order, standards of admission to membership being the first one and doctrinal standards being the last for which the young church will assume complete responsibility.

Self-Support

It cannot be over-emphasized that, regardless of the social and economic standards of the people, it should be understood that they are able to bear this responsibility unaided from the beginning. It includes:

Salaries and Support of the National Workers. The amount of these salaries should be decided by the infant church. The people themselves are in a far better position to know how much it takes to support an individual than does the foreign missionary and the salaries coming from national sources will on that account be much lower. These need not necessarily be paid in money. In some countries money is too scarce and the people too poverty-stricken to be able to pay in money. The setting apart of grains and other foods, or even of parcels of land for cultivation for the support of the minister or church leader, is a common practice. In return, these men are expected to render service for whole or part time, according to the local needs. Sometimes earnest young Christian men are found who gladly volunteer to give their services free until the churches are able to take on the support of the one who ministers to their spiritual needs. It is found to be inevitable that when the mission or missionary in charge begins by furnishing these salaries, it is a long struggle before the churches concerned are ready and willing to undertake that responsibility themselves.

Erection and Maintenance of Church Buildings and Property. This matter will be considered later, but it is sufficient at this point to say that it is often a temptation to begin a church with a building rather than with people. In the New Testament there is not one reference to church buildings or church property. There are, however, on the other hand a number of references to the "church in the house of" followed by the names of leading Christians in the various cities (Rom. 16:5; I Cor. 16:19; Col. 4:15; Philemon 2). The Scriptural example as well as experience in some mission fields would indicate very strongly that church buildings should be erected as needed by the local congregation, not by the missions. Only when this method is recognized as the normal procedure can the church be regarded as indigenous.

Expenses Involved in Carrying on the Essential Activities of the Church. This includes light and heat, janitor service, evangelism of all kinds, and the Sunday school. As long as a church, or group of churches, is dependent upon missions or on foreign sources for any item of its current budget or expenses, it is not self-supporting. Until it has reached that stage, it cannot be regarded as properly established, and the goal of the missionary not yet reached.

SELF-PROPAGATION

The winning of others to faith in the Lord Jesus Christ and to membership in the church includes all forms of evangelistic efforts, both at home and abroad. In all of these it should be understood that *every member bears a part and shares in this responsibility*. The importance and fruitfulness of personal work as the normal activity of each member cannot be over-emphasized. Careful surveys at home have shown beyond question that the one sure way of building up a church is through the consistent personal work of its members. The same thing has been proved again and again in the foreign mission field. In Korea it has always been expected that each believer should do his part as a personal witness to the gospel and to the blessing which it has brought into his own life. During my twenty-five years in Korea, in answer to questions put to them, thousands of candidates for baptism invariably gave evidence of this sort of personal work. It should be understood that unless a person's faith is real and vital enough to enable him to speak to others about the Lord and what He has done for him, that person is not ready to assume the responsibilities of full membership in the church.

On those fields where there is little entertainment and books are comparatively rare, conversation plays a great part in the life of the people. Speaking to others about any and every subject is not uncommon. Any new article or personal experience is a natural topic of conversation. Again and again when I have asked new Christians whether they speak to others about the Lord Jesus Christ and their new-found faith, their reply has been, "How would it be possible not to speak of Him and of what He has done for me?" When it is the normal thing for every believer to engage in personal evangelism, not only does the local church show steady and substantial growth, but it is a very easy matter to awaken interest and prayer and even financial support on behalf of preaching the gospel in more distant places.

These three important elements in the building up of an indigenous church—self-government, self-support, and self-propagation—go hand in hand. The average member has little desire to make contributions to the work of the church until he knows that he has a part in deciding how that money will be used and where it will be spent. Not until he feels that he has a share in the government of the church can he consider it is his and have a strong desire to tell others about it. Only as each one of these three functions is actually operating can any church become a "going concern," maintained by its own members in a constructive and fruitful manner. For this reason, therefore, when a missionary finds that his project has become entirely self-governing, self-supporting, self-propagating, and is reaching out to the evangelization of the entire district, then he can feel that his efforts in planting a live and vigorous church have been successfully completed.

QUESTIONS FOR DISCUSSION

1. Give a good definition of an "indigenous church."
2. Discuss the importance and place of self-government in the life of a church and name two tendencies concerning which care should be exercised in the establishment of a new church.
3. Discuss the important matters for which each church must assume responsibility before it can become fully self-governing. Suggest additions which could be made to the list given.
4. Discuss the various items for which the young church must take responsibility if it is to be truly self-supporting.
5. In what way does the individual member bear responsibility in order to make the church self-propagating? Discuss methods by which members can be led to realize and accept this responsibility.
6. Discuss the relationship between self-government, self-support and self-propagation.

CHAPTER III

FIXED FACTORS IN FOREIGN MISSIONS

ONLY A CASUAL examination of the work of foreign missions in various countries, even in different parts of the same country, is necessary to reveal striking contrasts in the stages of development reached. In some places, after decades of arduous labor by missionaries, there is very little to show in the way of self-supporting, self-governing, and self-propagating churches. The opposite is true in other places where the gospel has entered only comparatively recently and yet has brought about amazing results. Lives have been transformed and a strong indigenous church has been established. To understand and explain the varying degrees of development, it is helpful to analyze the various factors involved.

As we look into the work of missions, we at once realize that there are two that we might call *fixed* factors and *two variable* factors.

Under the heading of Fixed Factors are included two which are relatively fixed—at least they were until the last few decades. These can be referred to as the *message* and the *messengers*.

THE MESSAGE

The message is of course the gospel of Jesus Christ as Saviour and Lord. It is the historic message of the church which the apostles were commissioned by the Lord to preach and for the proclamation of which He promised them the power and presence of the Holy Spirit (Acts 1:8). To a very large extent, until within quite recent years, those who have been sent as missionaries have been faithful to this great historic body of doctrine, although various emphases have been placed upon it by different denominations. The varying conditions of life, represented both in those who preached and in those to whom they preached, have also produced some variation in the presentation of the great Christian doctrines. Nevertheless, the gospel message has been faithfully proclaimed with but little change down through the centuries. Unhappily, within the last few decades, owing to the inroads of Modernism in the churches of the homelands, this is no longer true, and men and women have been sent out who deny many of those things which have been regarded as the fundamentals of our faith. This has introduced a new and complicating factor in the whole work of foreign missions, and it must be very carefully considered in a future evaluation of the work.

THE MESSENGERS

What has been said of the uniformity of the message naturally cannot be equally true concerning the messengers. There have been a number of outstanding leaders who have been men and women of brilliant intellect, forceful personality, keen vision, and indomitable courage; and there has been a small minority whose temperament and general outlook and attitude have hindered their influence and accomplishment. Nevertheless, the messengers as a whole have been earnest and intelligent men and women, many of high educational attainments. Thoroughly consecrated to the Lord, they have been those whose theological viewpoints and general temperament, within certain generally recognized limits, have been in general on a standard pattern. They have gladly forsaken the comforts and joys of home and friends and have gone forward ready to live under conditions which, except for the sustaining power of the Lord Himself, would have been unendurable. The vast majority have faced these conditions cheerfully, and in their homes have established little oases of Christian life and grace in the vast deserts of paganism and idolatry. Each of these centers has become a lighthouse from which has shone out into the darkness of heathenism the light of the glory of the gospel of God as seen in the face of Jesus Christ.

QUESTIONS FOR DISCUSSION

1. What are the two fixed factors in all mission work?
2. Discuss and summarize what you should consider to be the message of the missionary to the pagan world.
3. Discuss the necessary qualifications for a successful missionary.
4. Name outstanding missionaries and show in what way they possessed these qualifications.

Chapter IV

VARIABLE FACTORS IN FOREIGN MISSIONS

—THE RECIPIENTS

IN ADDITION to what we have termed the fixed factors are the two variable factors which we might speak of as the *recipients* and the *methods*. Under these there are a bewildering assortment of conditions and circumstances, all of which have their reactions in the results of the proclamation of the gospel message.

THE RECIPIENTS

The recipients are those to whom the gospel is preached; they are people of every type. Let us consider a few of their differences.

Intellectual Attainments. The gospel is being preached to peoples of every degree of intellectual attainment. Tremendous difficulties have been faced by workers among aboriginal tribes of various countries, who have had no alphabet or literature of their own. Pioneer missionaries have learned many of their languages, reduced them to writing, translated and published the Scriptures and other books, and then taught the people to read in their own languages. More of this work is being carried on today probably than ever before. With the renewed interest in exploration and in pioneer evangelization, many new peoples and tribes whose existence was previously unknown are being reached. Concerted efforts are being made by a devoted company of men and women who have received special training in linguistics to push out among these tribes with the gospel, making it available to them in their own languages. Africa and Latin America today are the fields where the greatest amount of this work still remains to be accomplished.

At the other extreme are the highly educated and civilized nations, possessing their own languages and literatures, written either in alphabetical style or, as in the case of China, in the age-old and very complicated ideographs, needing years of study to master. Between these two extremes are peoples of every conceivable stage of intellectual development and thought patterns. To adjust themselves, missionaries have become intimately acquainted with these peoples only after long and arduous wrestling with the native languages and methods of thought—after years of consecrated and prayerful effort.

To some of these peoples it has been comparatively easy to make known the gospel of Jesus Christ, while to others the thoughts and ideas contained in the gospel have been so far removed from their experience that it has been difficult to find words and phrases to convey the message. These varying conditions have introduced complex educational problems, which the missions have sought to solve in many different ways.

Religions. Here again conditions are just as bewildering in their variety as was shown above. At the one extreme stand those powerful, well-organized, exclusive and militant religions which from the outset have furnished keen opposition to the work and the progress of the gospel. The outstanding one is Islam, the religion of the prophet Mahomet. While it is one of the three great monotheistic religions of the world, it worships only a caricature of the God of the Christians. Its followers have always been unyielding in their opposition to Christianity. As a result, missionary efforts in Mohammedan lands have been very meager in comparison with what has been accomplished elsewhere. In recent years in Japan the old national religion of Shinto was used effectively by the military party to hold back the advance of Christianity, especially since when in the hands of ruthless and unprincipled men, it gave them opportunities for bitter persecution and torture in enforcing their demands.

At the other end of the scale are the weak, unorganized, nonexclusive religions which have been unable to control the thinking of the people and which have had little with which to effectively oppose the proclamation of the gospel. In regard to this matter, one thing which we need to remember is the nonexclusive nature of many religions. For example, in the Orient it is quite common to find a man who is a follower of Confucianism, of Taoism, and of Buddhism all at the same time. The temple to which he goes, or the religion to which he looks on any given occasion, will depend largely upon his need at that moment. More than once Japanese officials have charged Christian missionaries with being narrow-minded, stating that they themselves were Shintoists on one day of the week and did obeisance to the sun goddess, and on Sundays they were Christians and went to church! They could not understand the unwillingness of Christian missionaries to adopt a similar view of compromise, of "broad-mindedness," whereby they too could honor Shinto deities in the name of patriotism on one day of the week and worship their own God at other times.

In practically all non-Christian countries, whatever the so-called national religions may be, in the minds of all there is a sub-stratum of animism underlying every belief and religious concept. Accordingly, even though a man is a worshipper of Confucius, or Buddha, he is nearly always a worshipper of spirits of one kind or another, with which he believes the unseen world is densely populated. While he has tablets or images of the well-known deities in his home, there will also be found somewhere about the place a bag of grain or a bundle of leaves, as the case may be, in which the spirit of his house or kitchen is supposed to reside. He will also from time to time take part in the worship of the spirit of the house site, or the spring, or the village, or some nearby mountain stream; and this belief and worship will in no way affect his adherence to the deities of the religion to which he makes his public profession.

Social Customs and Developments. During the past centuries various social practices have grown up which have greatly affected the thinking and development of various peoples. All these have their bearing on the presentation of the gospel. In those countries where ancestor worship is observed, in the clan or family resides the seat of authority and the individual has little liberty of choice or decision. Again, in every land where the gospel has not been proclaimed woman's place in society is very low. In some lands baby girls are considered hardly worth naming, and go through most of their lives known as the wife of so and so, and later as the mother and finally the grandmother of the eldest grandson. They are married off by their parents without any consultation whatever and become part of the family into which they marry and are little more than slaves to their mothers-in-law. Until comparatively recent years they were therefore considered quite unworthy of education and their only purpose in life was to cook and bear children for their husbands. In countries like Arabia and Mongolia where the people are largely nomadic, living in tents and moving from place to place, the conditions under which the gospel must be preached are entirely different from those in countries where cultures have been settled for centuries in towns and cities.

Economic and Industrial Development. Another of the variable factors which greatly affects the preaching of the gospel is the economic and industrial development of the people. In Africa, where the people for centuries have been living under primitive conditions and have practically no knowledge of agriculture or carpentry, special instruction along these lines has proved very beneficial. It was essential in order that living conditions could be raised to a point where Christian homes could be established and health maintained under fairly normal conditions. In many mission fields the introduction of modern methods of agriculture and better strains of seed and livestock has greatly improved the living conditions of the Christians and has done much for the development of self-support. In Korea, in an apple-growing district, one missionary who was formerly an experienced agriculturist, used to attend the country Bible conference and taught the men who came there for Bible study how to control the attacks of the borers, which were creating havoc in the orchards. As a result of this additional instruction at the Bible conferences, three or four churches, previously unable to support pastors, in a very short time were able to raise successfully the support of their own ministers. In the great industrial centers of India, China, and Japan, the missions have the problem of reaching with the gospel message thousands of men and women employed therein. Often these people spend years at a time inside the great factories, almost completely shut away from normal living conditions.

National Traits and Temperament. Each nation and people, during the course of centuries, has developed its own particular national temperament or characteristic. Many of these traits are clearly manifested in the religious life of the people. India, where there are more gods than there are people, has produced a number of religions. Philosophic mysticism, which is so characteristic of Buddhism, is found in the thinking of many—although as recent events have clearly shown, it can be easily cast aside and forgotten in wild excesses of bloodshed and cruelty. Opposite these are the Arabs, having a fatalistic and often ruthless way of looking at life. This has found its clear expression in the religion of Mohammed. This religion has for centuries exerted an overwhelming influence on its adherents. Even in peoples as closely related geographically as China and Korea and Japan, the national characteristics of each result in different approaches and different reactions to the gospel message. All of these matters should be carefully studied in order that the Christian message be the most effectively presented to the people in the area under consideration.

QUESTIONS FOR DISCUSSION

1. Discuss some of the linguistic problems which every foreign missionary must face, particularly those found in pioneer work and among illiterate peoples.
2. Name the great religions of the world, placing them in order of their influence and opposition to the spread of the gospel.
3. Name and discuss social customs which have had a marked influence on the missionary methods employed in the areas where they prevail.
4. Discuss various ways in which economic and industrial development has affected the proclamation of the gospel.

CHAPTER V

VARIABLE FACTORS IN FOREIGN MISSIONS

—THE METHODS

THE SECOND of the two variable factors is that of the methods used in mission fields. In response to the widely varying conditions of the people, some of which have been briefly referred to in the preceding chapter, there has been a corresponding variety in the way in which missions and missionaries have adapted their program to meet the needs of the people. As might be expected, in countries like Africa and India especially, where the economic level of people is very low, great emphasis has been placed on industrial work and industrial schools. Tremendous efforts have been made to improve the living conditions, especially of the Christians. Among these, notable examples are the great industrial enterprises carried out by Dr. Laws in Livingstonia, Africa, and by Dr. Sam Higginbotham in his leper colonies and agricultural work in India.

In India and Arabia where women are shut away from public life, and after marriage rarely go out of the homes of their husbands, zenana work has been carried on by women missionaries and their national co-workers. Here they spend much time visiting the secluded quarters of the women, presenting to them personally the claims of the Lord Jesus Christ and His gospel. It has been necessary in China, India, and in the Near East, in many cases, to establish separate hospitals for women, because those of the upper classes would not be willing to receive treatment in places where men patients are also accepted.

In Japan, which is one of the most literate countries in the world, some outstanding work has been done in newspaper evangelism, through which a surprisingly large number of men and women living in isolated communities have been reached. By correspondence with them and sending them Testaments and specially-prepared booklets and tracts, many have been won to faith in Christ Jesus. Japan, which has made such great strides during the past fifty years in adopting Western civilization, has large government hospitals; but the tight governmental restrictions upon foreign physicians resulted in the suspending of all mission medical work there. The exceptions are the great St. Luke's Hospital in Tokyo and one or two leper colonies. Even there, though, the medical work proper is carried on by Japanese physicians.

Leper colonies have been founded by the missions in nearly all those countries where leprosy is found and have been a fruitful branch of the work; for the condition of the lepers has made them especially open to the appeal of the gospel, with its message of comfort and hope; and thousands of these unfortunate people have been won to faith in the Lord Jesus Christ.

In China one of the characteristic forms of work has been that of the street chapels. In the many towns and cities it has proved to be most effective to rent shops in the markets and business streets, where for hours each day both missionaries and Chinese evangelists preach the gospel. Aided by the use of pictures and illustrations, in between sessions of preaching, these workers have been able to answer questions and enter into discussion with those interested. In this way a great evangelizing work has been carried on.

While these varying conditions of the people have resulted in various types of mission work, other factors have also affected the mission methods used.

FINANCIAL RESOURCES

As might be expected, nearly all specialized forms of mission work require the increased use of funds. The work of foreign missions has never received more than the minimum amount necessary to carry it on in the face of tremendous needs, both spiritual and physical, of the people to whom the gospel has been taken.

RESTRICTED EFFORTS

In spite of encouraging results obtained by some missions in various educational, medical, and other institutional activities, some missions have felt led to restrict their efforts to what is usually known as "evangelistic work." In view of the great expense, in funds and in missionary personnel, as well as the difficulty in securing well-qualified workers, they have felt forced to confine their activities to the preaching of the gospel and the establishment of churches, doing only the minimum of medical and education work.

ALERTNESS IN THINKING THROUGH PROBLEMS

Missions as well as individual missionaries differ in the way they are alert in thinking through problems of organization and adaptation which will meet constantly changing conditions. Some have been content to follow pioneer methods, in spite of vast changes in the lives and thinking of the people among whom they are working. Others have adapted their methods to fit new conditions and increased the variety and scope.

This discussion of the various methods of mission work, although very brief and inadequate, should make it clear that mission methods should fluctuate, in accordance with two particular factors.

The first of these factors is the change in political, economic, and social conditions of the people. Greater changes have occurred in the lives of nations since the close of World Wars I and II than had previously taken place in centuries. An entirely new set of conditions and problems to be faced by the missionary has arisen. With a sudden inrush of Western ideas in the Far East, the relation, for instance, between the sexes, has undergone revolutionary changes. Until very recent years, in many Oriental lands, a girl of twelve or thirteen was not supposed to have conversation with or be seen by men until after she had been married. Because of that, in some countries it was necessary to have curtains down the center of the churches, separating the men and boys from the women and girls. Co-education, except in the lowest grades, was absolutely unheard of. Now those are all things of the past. Boys and girls study together in high school and university, play tennis, and enjoy games and social relaxation together.

Industrial development and the resulting economic changes in nearly every important mission field have suddenly affected the living conditions of many people. In some cases this has been beneficial; in others the opposite is true. The sudden introduction of motor buses and street-car systems has brought many girls from the seclusion of their country homes into public life as conductors and fare collectors. Thousands of others have been pressed into service as waitresses in the cafes and restaurants which have sprung up like mushrooms in the large cities. These almost over-night changes have brought about such a revolution in the thinking of people that many tragedies have resulted, and accordingly many methods of mission work have had to be changed completely.

The second of these factors is that of the development of the work of the missions themselves. With the influx of Western ideas and a tremendous increase in national self-consciousness among the people, there has come into being a different relationship between the national Christians and the missionaries. This has necessitated new plans in the work. In the main it has meant a far greater participation in the government of the churches and an increasing interest on the part of the national Christians in the conduct of the church work. This has been a healthy development. In some areas it has meant heartaches for missionaries, who have been forced to give up positions of authority they had long held and had regarded as their own by inalienable right. In other fields far-sighted missionaries had from the beginning made arrangements for turning over this responsibility just as soon as the national Christians were ready. As the latter policy has been practiced, there has been greater efficiency in the work and friction or anti-foreign feeling has been avoided.

One of the outstanding developments in World War II was the "streamlining" of the courses of training. Notable among these has been the work done in language study in the various universities established by the government. In a comparatively short time young men and women have been given a grounding in languages which previously had required years of study. In missionary circles the Wycliffe Translators have made a notable contribution in the scientific approach to language study. They have developed the recognition of the various tones and sounds for the student to reproduce, have greatly shortened the breaking-down of the grammar of a given language. These developments have encouraged some to feel that in the near future similar great advances may be made in training national Christians to take over more rapidly the responsibility for the whole program of establishing the indigenous church.

Certainly mission boards and committees, as well as individual missionaries, by very reason of the critical conditions facing the Christian movement throughout the world, should be expected to give much prayerful thought to speeding up their work. They should carefully consider adapting policies now in use in order to make them increasingly effective. Under the guidance of the Holy Spirit they may find a new efficiency that in the space of a comparatively few years will enable them to do what previously had taken decades or even centuries to accomplish. This will require a new emphasis and the goal of mission work will be the planting of an indigenous church.

QUESTIONS FOR DISCUSSION

1. Discuss the development of industrial work in foreign missions, giving illustrations of what contributions it has made both to the life of the people and the development of the church.
2. Give illustrations of the way in which special social customs or economic conditions have resulted in specialized types of missionary activity.
3. For what two reasons should we consider that missionary policies and methods are inevitably in a fluid state?
4. Discuss how adaptability should become a qualification for a successful missionary in view of the conditions mentioned in this chapter.

In the discussion of these questions, if a specific mission field is considered, then concrete illustrations should be given showing changes in the life and thinking of the nationals and what missionary methods have resulted therefrom.

CHAPTER VI

THE HOLY SPIRIT AND MISSIONS

THE VALUE of using the New Testament as a textbook on missionary methods has been increasingly realized in recent years. It is remarkable how it throws light on problems which are common today to all mission fields.

A careful study of the Book of Acts and the Pauline Epistles, with a view to ascertaining the way in which the foreign missionary enterprise was begun in the Apostolic age, will reveal at once that the moral and social conditions of the people were similar to those in foreign mission fields today. With the same Holy Spirit to guide in the world-wide proclamation of the gospel, similar results can be expected.

PLACE OF THE HOLY SPIRIT IN THE FOREIGN MISSION ENTERPRISE

The book which we call the Acts of the Apostles very appropriately might be called the Acts of the Holy Spirit. In every incident the Holy Spirit is seen to be the active Agent and the directing influence in spreading the gospel.

PROMISED EQUIPMENT OF THE SPIRIT

In Acts 1:8 is found the promise of the Spirit made by the Lord Jesus Christ to His disciples, to equip them for their task of witnessing from Jerusalem to "the uttermost parts of the earth." For this world-wide task they could be prepared only by receiving a new power which the Holy Spirit would give them. In Peter's great sermon on the Day of Pentecost, he refers to the coming of the Holy Spirit as the fulfillment of the prophecy of Joel, who foretells the outpouring of God's Spirit upon His people, causing them to prophesy (Acts 2:17, 18).

ENABLING FOR PROCLAMATION

Various references are found to the Holy Spirit's enabling the apostles in the proclamation of the gospel in accordance with the promise of the Lord Jesus. In the second chapter they spoke with tongues "as the Spirit gave them utterance" (Acts 2:4).

38

Peter, "filled with the Holy Spirit" (Acts 4:8), spoke with boldness before the Sanhedrin, witnessing to the resurrection of the Lord Jesus Christ. Through that same power he and the others witnessed before the people. Stephen also spoke with such wisdom and authority from the Spirit that those who sought to oppose him were unable to withstand the power of his witness (Acts 6:10).

SUSTAINING FOR MARTYRDOM

In his victorious death, as the first Christian martyr, Stephen was filled with the Holy Spirit and in the hour of testing, "saw the glory of God and Jesus standing on the right hand of God," and triumphantly prayed for the forgiveness of those who were stoning him to death (Acts 7:55-60).

DIRECTING IN THE PROCLAMATION OF THE GOSPEL

The Holy Spirit on several occasions is seen to be the directing Agent in the proclamation of the gospel, both in regard to the decisions made concerning policy, and also concerning the *routes* the Apostles took and the *places* in which they witnessed. At the time of the great Apostolic conference in Jerusalem, when the questions arose as to what was necessary for salvation, particularly in respect to Gentile Christians, the council reached a unanimous decision. In the words of the document sent to the churches, "For it seemed good to the Holy Spirit and to us" (Acts 15:28), they revealed their consciousness that they had been guided by Him in that momentous decision—often called the Magna Charta of Christian Liberty. As they reached this decision, which changed the church from being a select Jewish society to a world-wide brotherhood, they were very conscious that their conclusion had been reached under the Holy Spirit's direction. He had enlightened their minds on this subject of such tremendous importance, and the unanimity of their judgment was another proof of His presence with them.

Not only was His guiding influence made manifest in this great question of church policy, but it was equally seen in the program of foreign missions. It was at His command that Philip left his fruitful work in Samaria to go down into the desert between Jerusalem and Gaza (Acts 8:26), where he had his memorable experience with the eunuch of Ethiopia and led him to the Lord. Philip was used by the Spirit in both these important steps which were preparing the apostles in

Jerusalem for the commencement of their world-wide proclamation of Jesus Christ.

Later on, in Paul's second great missionary journey, Luke relates, "And they went through the region of Phrygia and Galatia, having been forbidden of the Holy Spirit to speak the word in Asia; and when they were come over against Mysia, they assayed to go into Bithynia; and the Spirit of Jesus suffered them not" (Acts 16:6,7). "And when we had seen the vision, straightway we sought to go forth into Macedonia, concluding that God had called us to preach the gospel unto them" (Acts 16:10). These verses clearly indicate that the Holy Spirit had a very definite plan in the program of foreign missions and in the order of the places in which the gospel was to be preached. Just as He directed His servants in those early days, leading them to Europe instead of Asia, where Paul apparently was bent on going, so also in the days since then He has had a definite and exact program and purpose for each of His servants whom He commissions and sends out as ambassadors of Christ.

It was also the Holy Spirit who gave Peter the direct command to go with the men to the house of Cornelius, the Roman centurion in Caesarea (Acts 10:19,20), where for the first time the gospel was preached to a group of Gentiles. As Peter, under the direction of the Holy Spirit preached to them, to his amazement the Spirit came upon them with the same phenomenon which had characterized His coming upon the apostles on the Day of Pentecost, for they, too, "spoke with tongues" (Acts 10:46).

CALLING AND COMMISSIONING THE WORKERS

It was the Holy Spirit who said, "Separate me Barnabas and Paul for the work whereunto I have called them" (Acts 13:2). This verse marks the beginning of the foreign missionary enterprise of the church, and the Holy Spirit was the impelling force which initiated this great task. He has been the impelling force ever since down through the long history of foreign missions. It is He who has put the burning desire into the hearts of the thousands of young men and women who have felt called of God to go forth to the ends of the earth with the message of salvation. It is also He who has given to the sending churches the vision of the great heathen world with its appalling need and has awakened them to their responsibility toward those who have volunteered to go. Again it is the Holy Spirit who has been the directing Agent in the giving and the praying of the home churches, to sustain these representatives during their long years of service in the dark and lonely places to which the Lord has sent them.

Not only does the Holy Spirit call; He also commissions. "So they [Barnabas and Paul] being sent forth by the Holy Spirit, went down to Seleucia; and from thence they sailed to Cyprus" (Acts 13:4). The statement that these men, whom the Lord so signally honored by sending them as the first missionaries, were "sent forth by the Holy Spirit," would indicate both the assurance and the urge of which they must have been deeply conscious as they set sail from the port of Antioch. When anyone leaves friends and homeland and starts out for distant places at the call of the Lord, he must be tremendously conscious of the need for the Spirit's presence and power. This is the assurance which only the Holy Spirit can give to those whom He is commissioning for His service. That assurance never fades from the hearts of any whom the Lord sends out today, any more than it faded from the minds or experience of those early missionaries. It is a continual source of joy and confidence to know—regardless of the difficulties, hardships, disappointment, isolation, and loneliness—that He who gives the command, gives also the enablement and is therefore under His hand for blessing.

Confirming the Word

The Book of Acts is full of incidents showing how the Holy Spirit accompanied His servants as they went forth in obedience to Him. In various ways He confirmed the word which they spoke, making it real and alive and powerful to those to whom they witnessed. This was true of Peter's witness at Caesarea (Acts 10:44; 15:8), and was equally true on numerous occasions in the experience of the Apostle Paul. On his first missionary journey, as he was preaching in Pisidian Antioch, we read, "And as the Gentiles heard this, they were glad, and glorified the word of God; and as many as were ordained to eternal life believed. And the word of the Lord was spread abroad throughout all the region" (Acts 13:48,49). The hearts of the apostles must have been overjoyed when they saw that the gospel which had brought such wonderful results in Jerusalem and Judea and Antioch was bringing the same results in the great pagan centers on their missionary journeys. The many miracles of healing, both of body and soul, wrought through the proclamation of the gospel and the power of the Holy Spirit, and the many churches established during Paul's three great missionary journeys, are all marks of the confirmation of the Word by the Spirit of God.

Sustaining the Church

Not only is the presence and power of the Holy Spirit manifested to His messengers, but it is also seen in those who have been won to the Lord through the witness of His servants. After a time of bitter persecution following the martyrdom of Stephen, Luke records, "So the church through all Judea and Galilee and Samaria had peace, being edified; and, walking in the fear of the Lord and in the comfort of the Holy Spirit, was multiplied" (Acts 9:31). The young churches in mission fields often receive in a remarkable degree the comfort of the Holy Spirit.

The way in which He enables the new believers to rejoice in tribulation and to take joyfully the spoiling of their goods is another characteristic of the early church being duplicated in the young churches on the mission fields today. It is one of the gracious ways in which the same Holy Spirit confirms the faith of "little children" and at the same time uses them as witnesses, often to the conviction and conversion of those who have bitterly persecuted them. In the same way it is the Holy Spirit who is the active Agent in the organization of the churches, when in a spirit of prayerfulness and dependence upon Him they select their officers and leaders. As Paul reminded the elders at Ephesus on his farewell visit with them, "Take heed unto yourselves, and to all the flock, in which the Holy Spirit hath made you bishops, to feed the church of the Lord, which he purchased with his own blood" (Acts 20:28).

These are but some of the passages in the Book of Acts which reveal the place of the Holy Spirit in the work of foreign missions. A careful reading of that book will reveal others. Similarly, a study of the history of foreign missions will show therein a remarkable parallel to the Book of Acts as God's servants have gone forth in obedience under the leadership of the Holy Spirit. In dependence upon Him, they have carried on the proclamation of the gospel; and only as they have worked under that divine leadership have they been enabled to accomplish great achievements against fearful odds. When God's servants seek to invade Satan's territory, which he has held inviolate for centuries, they must expect bitter opposition. They can go only in the confidence that "If God be for us, who can be against us?"

QUESTIONS FOR DISCUSSION

1. Discuss the work of the Holy Spirit in the call of Barnabas and Paul to the work of foreign missions, as recorded in Acts 13. What part does He have today in this calling of men and women to do this same work?
2. Discuss what constitutes a call to be a missionary—its reception, its confirmation, its responsibility.
3. To what degree should missionary candidates today look to the Holy Spirit for their own physical, mental, and spiritual equipment?
4. Should we today expect the Holy Spirit to direct missionary activity in a way similar to that recorded in Acts? Discuss how this guidance should be sought and obtained.
5. Show that the foregoing question has a practical bearing on the life of the missionary.

CHAPTER VII

THE PIONEER STAGE

THE MISSION STATION

THE FIRST STEP in beginning mission work in any new field is the establishment of a mission station or headquarters. Great care should be taken, for a mistake at this point will seriously hinder the future development of the work. The site is of very great importance; it should be in a center of government, if possible. In these days of international suspicion it is always of great advantage for the missionaries to be in a center where they can have access to and contacts with government officials.

Experience has often shown that it is usually very much easier to deal with higher government officials than with those of a lower rank. As a rule, they are more likely to be men who have had some contacts with the outside world and who therefore are interested in having more of the same. They are also far less likely to be influenced by local, temporary, and antagonistic conditions which might make things very difficult for the newly-established missionary work. There is far less likelihood of misunderstandings, when the sympathy or interest of a high government official is won. It has its effect in smoothing out problems and in predisposing many to listen with courtesy and interest to the "foreigner" and his message. This basic relationship deserves careful thought and much prayer, and is one which many foreign missionaries are likely to regard as unimportant.

To some whose one chief interest is the preaching of the gospel of Christ, spending time with courtesy calls on officials in an effort to win their respect and sympathy may seem an unfruitful occupation, if not a real waste of time. But the far-seeing missionary—pioneer or otherwise—will recognize his definite obligation to win the confidence and friendship of these officials, not only for the sake of the salvation of their souls, but also for the greater influence their sympathy will exert throughout the whole territory. The example of Paul's courtesy to Felix and Festus as he made his defense before them is one which should be followed by every foreign missionary. The future usefulness and the effectiveness of his work greatly depends upon it.

A mission station should also, where possible, be in a *center of education,* where the future leaders of the nation can be brought into contact with the gospel. The student class is usually one of the most open to new ideas. Where young people are being brought into contact with Western thought, they are the more ready to listen to the foreign missionary, as he presents the claims of the Lord Jesus Christ. In many countries today, some of the outstanding leaders of the churches are those who were won to Christ in their early years as students. Japan has been a notable instance of this. In the early days when foreign missionaries were allowed to reside only in the Treaty Ports and were unable to travel into the interior, a large portion of their time was given to the teaching of English, both in schools and in classes in their own homes. Scores of the young students reached in this way were won to Christ. In later years they became the leading pastors of the Japanese church or influential Christian laymen in the highest government circles and the industrial world.

A mission station, where possible, should also be in a *trade center;* especially in countries where modes of transportation are primitive this is of great advantage. People coming in from the surrounding territory to buy and sell goods can be reached through tract distribution and other methods. Each of these becomes an instrument for spreading the gospel, carrying it into distant parts without the missionary himself making the long and expensive journeys involved.

For the same reason, the mission station should be in a *center of communication.* When this is the case, contact can be kept by mail and cable with home offices in times of danger or when special problems arise. Supplies can be sent and received more easily; also contact can be kept up with the newly established churches in the outlying districts and the influence of the missionary thereby is rendered much more effective.

In addition to the above, a mission station should be established with the idea of its becoming a *Christian center,* a center in which the church itself shall be strongly established, becoming a model or an example for other churches as they develop in the surrounding district. It is only natural that where a missionary takes up his residence the church should become strong and should be looked upon as a leader by the others. For that reason, with the development of the work, it should become a center for Bible conferences and, where possible, for a short-term Bible institute, and later a long-term Bible institute, where the local leaders from the country churches can receive systematic instruction, which will prepare them the better for carrying on their work among the local groups of their charge. As things develop, where possible, Christian schools, and perhaps a Christian hospital, and other similar institutions will be established and in this way Christian influences of various kinds will be going forth in every direction. Among other exceedingly important things is a bookroom, where supplies of Bibles and hymn books will be kept in stock and also other Christian books and tracts, as they are translated and prepared for the upbuilding of the faith of those who are already Christians and for arousing interest in those who are as yet out of Christ.

Evangelism

In the pioneer stage of any field or mission station evangelism naturally is the outstanding need and the activity in which the foreign missionary will be chiefly engaged. This will mean in the first place widespread seed-sowing and extensive itineration. During this time the whole area should be visited and the gospel proclaimed in every possible way, by the distribution of tracts, by personal contacts, by visiting officials, by making friends, whenever and wherever opportunity offers and by getting to know the field with its special needs and its outstanding opportunities. The distribution of tracts and the sale of penny Gospels and small Christian books have been greatly used in some countries for the opening up of new territories and for the introducing of the gospel. As contacts are made and interested persons emerge, periodical visits will be made to their homes and time spent with them, winning their confidence and giving definite instruction, so that as soon as possible they may be led into the light.

Group Evangelism. As the country is traveled over and strategic places of promise are found, intensive evangelism must be carried on wherever interest has been shown, whether by open-air preaching in the market places or as in China and other countries, by the use of street chapels or tents. Where possible, work should be carried on by teams of missionaries and national Christians. Fairs and heathen festivals, where great crowds gather, have often afforded special openings for this work. It is worth while noting that none of the so-called great world religions, with the exception of Mohammedanism, has manifested the power or the desire to carry on an active witness and propaganda such as we usually associate with the gospel of Christ. It is always one of the definite evidences of the reality of regeneration in a man's heart that he manifests his readiness to go out and tell others of his new found faith and joy in the Lord. There is nothing that is more thrilling to the missionary, more effective in its impact on the heathen population, and more stimulating to the faith of the new convert than this public witnessing to what has taken place in his life through the acceptance of Jesus Christ as his Saviour and Lord. Similarly, there is nothing that better strengthens the bonds of fellowship and confidence between missionary and national than their going out together publicly to proclaim the gospel. This must be done to make a definite impact upon heathenism and to give a demonstration of the dynamics of the gospel as it works in the lives of those who have accepted it.

Personal Evangelism. Personal evangelism is the responsibility and the privilege of every missionary and it must be continual. Paul's message to Timothy, "Preach the word; be instant in season and out of season," is one that must be the motto of every truly evangelistic missionary. As is the case of every good salesman, he must take special pains to "sell himself" as a living demonstration of the gospel which he preaches; especially in pioneer work must particular care be taken in regard to the first impressions made on people in a new place. I can remember conversations with Korean Christians who told me the impressions they had received when meeting a missionary for the first time thirty years previous. Because of his newness to the country and its customs, he had failed to comply with Korean custom and had not removed his shoes on entering an inn where he was staying for a few hours. The unhappy impression received then remained with those men for years and was for a long time a barrier to their accepting Christ. The Reverend Dwight Malsbury, in Korea, by his own life and example, gave an unforgettable illustration of what can be accomplished by consistent and persistent personal evangelism. He made it his custom, when he was not teaching in his music classes, to spend his free time in the main streets of Pyengyang doing personal evangelism with the people as they came in from their country homes to market or were returning after transacting their business. During a period of some five years over 1800 people made a definite profession of accepting the Lord Jesus Christ as Saviour and so recorded their names as the result of that one man's efforts.

It is of importance in this connection to remember how greatly the future development of any church or the work in any given village will depend upon the character of the first converts won, for in many ways they will set the pace and the precedent for all who follow. Experience has proved again and again the great desirability, where possible, of winning as first converts, people from among the sturdy middle class. One or two families among such, humanly speaking, will guarantee the future growth of the work; whereas if people of the lower classes and illiterates are the first converts, it will be understood by many that the gospel is meant simply for such people and that therefore no self-respecting, well-to-do man would care to accept it. In the same way, if members of the upper class are first brought to faith in Christ, as a usual thing the lower strata of the population will have neither the inclination nor the confidence to associate with them in their newfound faith.

Medical Evangelism. A medical work carried on by consecrated doctors and nurses again and again has proved itself of inestimable value in winning confidence and in breaking down barriers of strangeness and timidity. The great mission field of Korea has often been said to have been opened by a lancet when Dr. O. R. Avison, the pioneer medical missionary, opened a boil from which one of the members of the Imperial family was suffering. The interested and unselfish care of the sick, as shown by a Christian physician, is almost unknown in heathen lands and even where more or less modern government hospitals have been established, patients continually marvel at the difference in the atmosphere and in the treatment which they receive from the hands of Christians in contrast with what they receive in government and pagan institutions. In Korea, in one mission station's territory alone, over seventy self-supporting, indigenous churches have been planted as a result of the evangelistic work carried on in one hospital. A regular part of the staff of that hospital was composed of three ordained ministers and three Bible women. One pair of these workers spent one month at a time doing personal work in the hospital, speaking to the patients and visiting with their friends and families who had come with them, and that was followed by two months out in the villages visiting the ex-patients who had returned to their homes, encouraging and building them up in their newfound faith and preaching to their relatives and friends and establishing groups of new believers. Oversight of these groups was continued until they had purchased or erected their own church building and were ready to make regular contributions to the salary of a minister who was in charge of other churches in the same district. Then they were turned over to the presbytery who assigned one of the men in that territory to minister to them. Every mission hospital where the doctors and nurses themselves have maintained a keen interest in personal work with the patients has been of untold value. It has opened the way for the entrance of the Word of God into the hearts of those who had heretofore been indifferent, if not hostile, to the gospel.

QUESTIONS FOR DISCUSSION

1. Discuss briefly important factors that should be kept in mind in the selection of a mission station, explaining the importance of each one.
2. Make a special study of Paul's policy in his choice of strategic centers for preaching the gospel and establishing churches.
3. Will the development of the mission station into a strong Christian center be likely to impede the church there from being established on an indigenous basis?
4. Discuss several types of evangelism in the pioneer stage of missionary work.
5. Study methods used by some of the great pioneer missionaries in the various mission fields.
6. Discuss the necessity and the possibilities of a missionary "selling himself" in order to win a sympathetic hearing for the gospel. This will include emphasis on carefulness to make "first impressions" favorable ones, and on learning local customs and etiquette.

CHAPTER VIII

THE ORGANIZING STAGE

HAVING MADE the initial contacts and having seen individuals come out of heathenism and accept the Lord, the next major step is that of gathering the new believers into groups and organizing them into churches. This is the stage in which first impressions are made in regard to church life and to the responsibilities and standards for Christian living on the part of the members. Precedents are set which will be of utmost importance in the future development of the work. In this stage it is easy for the missionary to make mistakes which will have lasting effect upon the growth of the church into a truly indigenous body. Special care must be taken along several lines.

RESPONSIBILITY FROM BEGINNING TO BE PLACED ON NEW CHURCH

Conducting Their Own Services. It is easy for a missionary, by always leading the services himself or having an evangelist do it, to start out the new believers with the feeling of dependence upon some outsider to lead their worship. In Korea I have often cautioned men who were going out to do pioneer evangelistic work in new villages to attempt to organize churches in two different places at the same time, if possible, so that at least every other Sunday the new believers would be left to themselves to conduct their own services entirely under their own leadership. Notably in Korea where the development of the church has been rapid, many of the national pastors, whether ordained or unordained, are in charge of anywhere from one to ten groups of believers or churches. The newer groups in the country villages, being small and weak, are quite unable to undertake alone the support of a pastor. They are therefore organized into circuits which are then placed under the pastoral charge of qualified men. This means that in some cases only once in several months will the minister in charge be able to conduct the Sunday services, and the local leaders will have to take care of the rest themselves. It is remarkable how rapidly the new converts will develop under the guidance of the Holy Spirit, when left to themselves in this way. Simple instruction must be given as to the meaning and the essential factors in worship in the different parts of the service. A booklet entitled "A Straight Road to Worship" has been prepared in the Korean language, which gives instructions to these local leaders as to the meaning of the various parts of the service and how preparation for each part can best be made, both on the part of the leader and of the congregation.

Maintaining Exemplary Christian Conduct. From the beginning, standards must be set and instruction given as to what constitutes Christian living. The necessity for maintaining these standards at all costs must be impressed upon the new believers, for as noted above, the training of these first converts will inevitably set the type for the future development of the church. One danger is that of allowing them to rely on the foreign missionary and upon his decisions rather than upon the leading of the Holy Spirit through the reading of the Word of God.

Experience in Korea and elsewhere has plainly shown that where clear-cut standards of Christian living have been set and maintained it has meant a strong testimony before the heathen population. It has also been an immeasurable source of power to the church itself in maintaining a high morale amidst persecution and discouraging circumstances. Besides this it has discouraged people from seeking to enter it, who had no serious purpose in their hearts.

As we shall see later, setting these standards will raise complex problems connected with ancient customs, which may have religious significance. It is evident that such questions can be settled only with much thought and prayer. Consultations and conferences together by missionaries and national Christians will eventually in most cases bring about a solution satisfactory to all.

A careful study and meditation on I John 2:24-27, which reads: "The anointing which ye received of him abideth in you, and ye need not that any one teach you; but as his anointing teacheth you concerning all things, and is true, and is no lie, and even as it taught you, ye abide in him," will do much to encourage the missionary to place much of this responsibility upon the national Christians rather than to seek to carry it all himself. In many churches in the mission field, as a regular thing, it is understood that all deacons and elders can naturally be called upon at any time to lead worship services on Sunday morning and evening or to take charge of the prayer meeting on Wednesday evening; and it is found to be a very helpful custom to call upon some of these officers to lead in prayer at all regular worship services of the church. It is also equally taken for granted that any of these officers will be ready, as called upon, to visit in the homes of the believers to encourage and to advise as may be needful, as well as to pray with and for the sick.

PREPARATION FOR ORGANIZATION OF CHURCHES

Experience has proved the value of instructing the new believers from the very beginning in the keeping of church rolls on which the names of all are kept from the time when they publicly profess their desire or decision to accept Jesus Christ as Saviour and Lord. A record of attendance is kept at all services, both on Sunday and during the week, so that from the beginning their responsibility to be present whenever the believers gather is impressed upon them. Similarly, from the first time that services are regularly held in a new village, the offering as an integral part of the service is stressed. Where the people are too poor to bring money, in its place they are taught to bring foodstuffs or grain. This latter is often carried in little bags which are emptied into a larger chest or left with one of the church leaders. It is not uncommon in Korea to see several bushels of grain brought in in this way each Sunday, especially by the women Christians who take a spoonful or so out of each day's ration for presentation to the Lord and are willing literally to eat that much less themselves in order that they may have a part in the support of His work. From the very beginning, therefore, of each group, church account books must be begun and a careful record kept of all that comes in, which must be regularly audited from time to time.

Systematic instruction of new believers must be carried on from the beginning. In some fields the rule is to receive new believers first as catechumens for a period of not less than six months, during which time training is given as to the meaning of faith in Christ, the duties of prayer, Bible study, church attendance, the observance of the Lord's Day, the meaning of redemption, and the great cardinal doctrines of the Church, together with simple instructions in daily living a Christian life. Later on, after another period of not less than six months, they are eligible for baptism, after having given satisfactory evidence before the minister or church officers as to the reality of their faith and an adequate understanding of the Christian doctrines, the sacredness of baptism and the Lord's Supper, and their responsibilities as church members, which in turn has been manifested by a consistent Christian life during this period. By this procedure many of those who professed to believe, without realizing the seriousness of the step or the obligations involved, are given time to come to a true knowledge of the truth. Those who fail to do so usually drop out before being examined for baptism.

Appointment of Temporary Officers. As each new group is formed, temporary officers are appointed by the missionary or pastor in charge, and these men and women are taught as to their responsibilities and duties, are counselled with each time new believers are admitted or new members enrolled. As church problems arise they are discussed and prayed over with these temporary officers, for the purpose of receiving their advice and viewpoint. These are invaluable to any missionary in pioneer work. This training gives them actual experience in guiding others along the paths of Christian instruction and living.

THE NEVIUS METHODS

The late Dr. Nevius, a missionary for many years under the Northern Presbyterian Mission in Shantung, China, inaugurated some principles in the early days which have very greatly affected the work in Korea from its beginning. Dr. Nevius spent a short time with several of the pioneer missionaries to Korea and gave them three outstanding principles which have formed the backbone of the policy, at least of the Presbyterian work in that country, which has been so remarkably successful. In brief, these principles were:

(1) The importance of setting high standards from the start in Christian conduct and of insisting upon a complete break with heathen customs before admission to church membership. Dr. Nevius said, in effect, "Do not make it too easy to become a Christian. Make the standards of Christian living so distinct from the heathen standards that there can be no question as to what faith in Christ stands for in the minds of any outsiders when they come into contact with Christians."

(2) Self-support from the very beginning, that no "foreign" money should be used in the salaries of church workers or in the erection of church buildings but that all should come from the resources of the people themselves.

(3) Thorough Scriptural indoctrination.

These three principles have been carried out in Korea as in but few other parts of the world. Some of the questions involved will be referred to later, but a very clear break has been insisted upon in regard to participating in ancestral sacrifices, in the use of drink, or the attendance at heathen festivals of any form, and also in regard to inter-marriage between Christians and non-Christians. A very strong emphasis has been consistently placed upon regular attendance at all church services and a strict observance of the Lord's Day, in cessation of all but necessary forms of work. Daily Bible reading and family worship have been widely stressed. When traveling in the country I have often been able to tell which were the Christian homes by hearing the hymns sung at family prayers.

In the matter of self-support, from the very beginning no mission funds have been used for ordained pastors' salaries and only seldom in the salaries of the unordained men who were carrying on the work of pastors among the newly organized groups. In exceptional cases, among the latter men who were in charge of the very small and weak new groups, temporarily up to one-third of their small salary was subsidized by the mission, but that was later completely stopped. Even the salaries of evangelists going out into unevangelized territory were not paid from mission funds and the responsibility of evangelizing their own people from the beginning has been held before the national church. Within twenty years of the beginning of the work, The Boards of Home and Foreign Missions of the Korean Presbyterian Church were established, which have consistently supported well-qualified ordained men in home and foreign mission work. In addition, the more than twenty presbyteries, as well as the local churches, have been doing a great work in sending out evangelists through their missionary societies and committees which are formed in every church when it is established.

Systematic teaching of the Bible has been one of the outstanding characteristics of mission work in Korea and is one of the secrets of its wonderful growth. This has been greatly aided by the fact that the Korean alphabet is one of the simplest in the world and can very easily be learned by even the most ignorant. Because of this, it has been a church rule that no one should be baptized under the age of fifty who has not learned to read. Not only has the simple alphabet been of great help to the growth of the church, but the rapid growth of the church with its interest in Bible study proved to be a great influence in regaining popular interest in the Korean alphabet, which had fallen into disrepute. Scholars and literati frowned on it as being too simple and were using the complicated Chinese ideographs; and women were considered as being too busy with household duties to have time to learn to read! Sunday school services often have the largest attendance of any service of the day and are usually held in three separate sections—for men, women, and children. This is done partly because of lack of space in church buildings and also because of the necessity for one member of the family always to remain at home to look after the house, in a land where locks and keys are very flimsy. Next to the Bible and the hymn book, the Sunday school quarterly is the best seller and is diligently read and studied. In addition, a great system of Bible conferences has been developed in which systematic Bible instruction is given. These conferences usually last from five to ten days and commonly consist of an early morning prayer service about daybreak, two hours of instruction in the morning, with an hour of devotions in between, one or two more hours of instruction in the afternoon; and then all those in attendance are expected to go out with tracts and do personal work, inviting people in for the evening service. The only textbook used is the Bible and each person brings a pencil and notebook and expects to receive an outline which he can take down and carry home with him for future reference and study. The Bible is studied by books and special courses are given on doctrine, prayer, the life of Christ, His birth and death, His miracles, and parables. In the larger district conferences often between 1,000 and 2,000 people are enrolled. Those in attendance are divided into groups, according to their status in the church: new believers, catechumens, young, middle-aged, and elderly baptized members, deacons, elders, and pastors. A small enrollment fee is charged to pay the expenses of light and heating as well as for entertaining guest speakers. Those who come in pay their own expenses, being housed either in school or Bible institute dormitories which may be available or in the homes of the Christians of the town. In 1937 the total attendance at the Bible conferences for the Presbyterian Church in Korea, which had a membership at that time of 130,000, was 170,000, and in the twenty-five years previous, only on three occasions had the total enrolled at Bible conferences fallen below the total baptized membership of the church.

In addition to the instruction at Sunday schools and these Bible conferences, is that given in the short-term Bible institutes which were established in all the mission stations. In these institutes, which were held for men and women separately, a carefully worked out course covering all sections of the Bible, together with courses in personal work, preaching, teaching, church history, and other subjects, was taught and examinations given at the close. These institutes run from one to two and a half months and here again the students pay all their own expenses and a small enrollment fee. In these the lay leaders of the local churches receive their instruction and in many cases the smaller country groups make it possible for some of their promising young men and women to attend by supplying them with the necessary few bushels of rice to eat while in school. The main purpose of the Bible institutes is the training for lay leadership and preparation for those planning to attend the theological seminary. Their influence in the development of the church has been of incalculable help.

Planning Future Development

In planning for the future development of the church in any one district, certain things must always be kept in mind. Among these will be first the needs of the whole area. Unless this planning is done, there is a grave danger of the missionary becoming "bogged down" in one place. If he becomes too much interested in the development of the group in his own mission station and becomes tied down in caring for it, not only are the needs of the larger area in danger of being forgotten, but the local group easily gets into the bad habit of looking to him for assistance so much that it fails to develop its own strength and initiative. I have visited in other mission fields where the missionaries have become regular pastors in charge of the established churches. Each man therefore had charge of one, or possibly two churches only, and spent his whole time in carrying on the regular pastoral duties, visiting the sick, and conducting weddings and funerals. His salary of course was paid by his mission, and those churches were thus relieved of that financial responsibility. On one occasion a Christian family moved to an outlying district and asked the missionary to come to visit them, using their home as a center in which to establish a new church.

The reply was that with two churches already under his charge he could not afford the time to minister in a third place. In the neighboring territory, under a different mission, each missionary had charge of from twenty-five to sixty churches, in which the pastoral care was carried on by unordained men who were being trained as pastors and were looking forward to being in full control when their theological education was completed and when the churches to which they were ministering were in a position to assume their support. In the one case the efforts and influence of each missionary were limited to one or two towns or villages, and there was no incentive for those churches to look for one of their own people to become their pastor, nor was there any real incentive given for young men to prepare themselves for church work, inasmuch as practically all the organized churches were already being taken care of by experienced missionary pastors. In the neighboring mission field, not only were the influence and efforts of each missionary spread over a wide area, but the manner in which the work was carried on was a stimulus to each church to develop to the point where it was able to assume the full support of its own national pastor, who would then give it his full time and attention. As that took place, more time and opportunity were given to the missionary to take part in forward evangelistic movements and in the organizing of new groups in other places, and thus provide new openings for young men to be trained in practical church work and to prepare themselves for the ministry. It was not until the first-mentioned district had been operating for about fifty years that its first national pastor was ordained and installed. But after about twenty-five years of work in the neighboring mission field, some seventy-five to one hundred ordained national pastors were in active service. From the beginning, definite and systematic prayer with the Christians for the needs of the whole district should be carried out in order to get them to realize their responsibility for their own people.

All institutions and organizations should be planned with the view that they will in time be taken over entirely by the national Christians and will cease to be in any sense foreign or mission institutions. This will mean in certain countries a simpler form, both of organization and of building, than those to which the missionaries are accustomed in their home lands. It is not wise nor fair to burden an infant church in a new country with the complex and heavy organization which has grown up over the course of years in the home lands. Neither does the fact that certain organizations have proved successful in this country necessarily prove them to be best-suited to the peoples of other lands, especially where standards of social life and education are widely different. The very fact that a mission erects an expensive, and, when judged by the standard of living of the people, an elaborate church building and very attractive to those in that vicinity, may easily prove to be a source of discouragement to Christians in other districts, who realize that they themselves can never hope to be able to duplicate any such structure. Still more, its foreign type of structure may definitely alienate it from their interest and sympathy.

In certain ritualistic denominations where emphasis has been placed on church architecture, altar cloths, robes, and the various mechanics of ritual, the simplicity of the gospel has sometimes been hidden and the whole movement has been given a setback by reason of what seems to the natives as a thoroughly foreign setting. While one can say that over-institutionalization and over-organization have been dangers in denominational missions, yet in many of the undenominational missions there has been a weakness due to insufficient foresight and planning in regard to organization. With the emphasis given to the proclamation of the gospel as the main purpose of the individual missionary and a corresponding lack of emphasis on planning and developing an indigenous church, the result has been large groups of believers being won; but because of a failure on the part of the missionaries to think through a well-integrated plan of church development, there has been a corresponding weakness and a noticeable slowness on the part of the church members to take their full share in the important matters of self-support, self-government, and self-propagation.

QUESTIONS FOR DISCUSSION

1. In connection with what two matters especially should full responsibility in general be placed upon the newly organized church groups?

2. What steps should be taken to help them in assuming this responsibility?

3. Discuss the wisdom of insisting on a period of instruction

and training for the new converts before admitting them by baptism into full membership of the church.

4. Discuss the Nevius principles—both as to their content and also as to their application in new groups of believers.

5. What dangers may be avoided by careful planning for the evangelization and development of the church in the whole area?

6. In what way will this planning affect institutions and organizations?

CHAPTER IX

TRAINING IN LEADERSHIP

IT IS IMPOSSIBLE to over-estimate the importance of training leaders, for on their training and calibre must depend
the future development of the indigenous church. In pioneer
stages, of necessity a major part of the missionary's time must
be given to widespread itineration and seed-sowing and both
public and personal evangelism, but after the pioneer stage has
been passed, the activities of a missionary should be increasingly
focused upon training future leaders. This is done both by
special instruction and by example. Just as soon as groups of
believers have been established, training classes should be organized, whether in the form of short-term Bible institutes or special
classes for the preparation and development of local leaders.
One thing that must be remembered is that each time a missionary can train and set at work a national, he is more than
duplicating himself and his own usefulness. The multiplication
of himself in the lives of others should be one of the main goals
of the missionary, with the understanding that he himself is
controlled by the Lord Jesus Christ. As yet no mass production
or assembly line methods for this work have been developed,
and it is a matter of personal influence and training more than
anything else that will bring the desired results.

We cannot over-emphasize the power of example in this
particular field. It is well known that in practically every
mission field the national leaders as they develop, especially in
the early stages, look to the foreign missionary as an example,
sometimes to an amusing degree. I have seen gestures, intona-
tions, and even mispronunciation of certain missionaries reflected in the men they have personally trained and whom they
have brought up in the faith. Paul on more than one occasion
in his Epistles writes to his friends, "Be ye imitators of us,"
not from any sense of pride or self-sufficiency, but of necessity;
for in Paul's time there were no books to tell people what a
Christian life was; neither were there any generally accepted
standards as to what Christian living meant, and therefore Paul
says to those who have accepted the Lord as their Saviour, "If
you want to know how to live and how to meet the issues which

you will face from day to day, imitate me and my colleagues, who have the guidance of the Spirit and then learn to look to Him yourselves for His direction in all matters." It is not only what the missionary says and does that is going to count but, even more, it is what he is in his own personal life that will have the greatest effect upon his co-workers. As he arranges for some of them to accompany him on evangelistic trips and upon visitations to churches, they are watching him and taking their cue from him in matters of courtesy, in treatment of the heathen, in answering questions from Christians and non-Christians, in dealing with cases of discipline, and in almost every detail, not only of church life but of Christian conduct.

In connection with this matter of training church leaders the absolute necessity of taking care in the selection of all one's associates from the very first is apparent. Even the choice of household servants is one in which this principle must be borne in mind. Whenever possible, all such should be Christians, for they will be the interpreters of the missionary and his home life to outsiders throughout the district. In Korea many of the young men who first started out with the missionaries as their country cooks or boys who attended them on their itinerating trips, during the course of years became pastors and influential men in the Korean Church. Traveling with the missionaries in the country and receiving from them tracts to distribute along the way, introduces them to the privilege of serving the Lord; and as night after night they hear the story of the gospel preached by the missionary and observe his personal work and that of those with him, they too begin to develop a taste for the same thing and very often become church officers, if not pastors and evangelists. I suppose it is the experience of every missionary that often he has been surprised by the number of the intimate details of his household and home life which have become a matter of common knowledge in the town. The kind and the number of the clothes he wears, the quality of the food and the dishes on the table, the way he treats his wife and children and the other servants, his ability to control his temper, and the hours he keeps, are all matters of consuming interest to the people in a strange land, and his servants are naturally eyes and ears for the village and report everything which they themselves observe to the advantage or disadvantage of the missionary, depending upon the understanding and tact which he displayed in the incident in question. This being the case, loyal and devoted Christian house servants add immeasurably to the influence and usefulness of a missionary, while dishonest and ungrateful ones usually hurt his influence and create misunderstandings and sometimes real opposition. It has often been said that a missionary has the privacy of the proverbial gold fish and no more!

SECRETARIES AND PERSONAL HELPERS

In a mission station in which a number of missionaries are working, it is sometimes possible to have one of the nationals as the secretary for all the workers and thus be a station secretary. At other times each missionary may have his own personal helper or secretary. In many cases these men have proved themselves invaluable. As they grow in experience it is possible for the missionary to send his secretary out in his place to visit churches where special problems have arisen. Such a man is also of great help in examining the rolls and auditing the accounts in the various churches as the work is beginning and before a system has been put into operation on the part of the local church or the presbytery itself for taking care of such matters. These men, because of their knowledge of the habits and customs of their own people, are able to give very helpful advice to the missionaries concerned, in regard to the attitude that they should take concerning specific problems or situations as they arise. They are of invaluable aid in writing a large part of the necessary correspondence between the missionary and his friends. Regular letters to the churches and other groups, containing suggestions for sermons and special exhortations, giving bits of church news and items of encouragement or reports on the general financial condition of the churches and presbytery or conference will prove to be a real stimulus to the faith and interest of members of the churches to which they are sent. These letters will do much also to bind together the various members and churches and to develop a feeling of solidarity as the realization comes that all are interested in each other and in the one great cause of the proclamation of the gospel.

As a missionary gets to know groups among whom he is working and as their confidence in and affection for him grow, he will find himself continually asked for advice and suggestions on subjects relating to practically every phase of church life and family and individual life. He will be consulted on matters of church quarrels, church debts, architecture, and the erection of church buildings, the care and registration of deeds, the organization of missionary societies, young people's societies, and the disbursement of funds and kindred subjects. When it comes to the lives and homes of the Christians themselves, they will discuss with him the matter of their own personal debts and how they can best arrange to defray them; they will constantly ask him for information as to where they can find the right kind of boys and girls for satisfactory sons-in-law and daughters-in-law; advice will be asked in regard to making a change of residence and where larger opportunities can be found in business, or perhaps advice as to the kinds of crops to plant, new methods of agriculture and a hundred and one other matters. On certain occasions where persecution is bitter, the missionary will be called on to interview some of the officials of the neighborhood, or some of the village leaders, if possible, to see how a better understanding can be brought about, and the opposition and persecution lessened. It is needless to say that if under these conditions a missionary has a wise secretary to help, to advise, and often to go in his place and act for him, his efficiency and his usefulness will be increased many times. Incidentally, for the secretary such work is splendid training, if he is looking forward to the ministry. Many young men of promise and earnest faith have started out in this way as a personal assistant or secretary to a missionary and developed into successful and efficient pastors.

Here again the importance of choosing a secretary wisely cannot be over-estimated. In certain localities where the wrong choice has been made, untold sorrow and heartache have resulted, and those chosen have been known to deceive the missionaries and use their position as a means of wielding influence in church decisions and in family problems in an utterly unauthorized way. This has not only made enemies for the missionary but has seriously hindered the growth of the church over comparatively wide areas.

In many mission fields women missionaries also have been very greatly assisted in their work by having Bible women as their personal helpers, who accompany them in their visits to the country churches, and help in arrangements for and teaching in Bible conferences. The employment of a secretary or helper on mission funds does not violate the principle of self-support, so long as his work is limited to that of making more efficient

the usefulness of a missionary or missionaries. This he accom-
plishes by assisting in correspondence, in preparations of sermons
and addresses, in advising with nationals concerning personal
or church problems, and by attending to necessary details of
the missionaries' work and thus freeing them for more important activities. He is not to be used as a pastor or an evangelist,
although on necessary occasions he may preach in the place of
the missionary.

Special Training of Church Officers

In the previous paragraphs we have been considering what
might be termed the "unofficial" and "indirect" method of training men and women, both by example and personal relationship,
and thus preparing them to take influential positions in the
churches. In addition to this, there should be specific training
for those who are going to be given responsibility in the churches
in an official way. This specialized training will vary in accordance with the form of government adopted and the qualifications for the various offices, as decided by the churches in question. But the following basic principles can be laid down.

Experience in Local Churches. As a new group of believers
comes into being, from the beginning one or more of these new
Christians, who show special promise or who are looked up to by
the others, are appointed as temporary local leaders, and upon
them necessarily must fall in large measure the responsibility
for leading the services and for the general oversight of their
own particular group. Usually at first they are appointed by
the missionary or pastor in charge, but as the number of baptized
members increases and they grow in faith, these men are elected
to their office by the baptized members of the group. On each
occasion, when the missionary or pastor visits that group or
church and examines members for enrollment as catechumens
or for baptism, the local leader sits in with him, listening to
the questions, and his advice and opinion should be asked on
each individual; for he knows their home life and their general
influence and testimony. He should be consulted therefore by
the missionary or pastor in charge of the district, in regard to
each one received into membership and he should be taught
how to write minutes so that from the beginning a permanent
record will be kept of all those joining the church and all decisions made in regard to matters of discipline or organization of
the Sunday school and the appointment of Sunday school

teachers. In this manner, from the very first he will understand that the responsibility of leading the church to a successful growth will rest upon him and those associated with him, either by appointment or by election. There is nothing that encourages more the spirit of self-respect and a desire to work for the church, than the consciousness fostered from the start that the church is in no way the property of the missionary or pastor in charge of that area, but is the possession of its members. It is a never-failing cause for astonishment to new missionaries and even to old ones, to see how ready people are to take over responsibility when it is given to them and how rapidly they develop under responsibility.

In the Orient, as in practically all mission fields, women in the past have had no place of authority and sometimes but little opportunity for self-expression. When they come to know Christ, however, and become part of the Church, immediately a new sense of the dignity of womanhood and its rights arises. Women's missionary societies and circles, which have always formed an integral part of every church in Korea, everywhere awaken a new spirit of service and of confidence on the part of their members. This was especially noticeable in Korea shortly before the outbreak of World War II, when the Japanese government was inaugurating a forward plan throughout Korea, with organizations in every village; in almost every area where there was a church, the Japanese officials asked one of the Christian women to act as president of the women's section. On a number of occasions I asked the officials the reason for their preference for Christian women. The invariable reply was that the Christian women were the only ones who knew how to conduct a public meeting. The experience which they had had in the churches and their missionary societies had given them not only a knowledge of how to do things but a poise which enabled them to hold the meetings in order and according to parliamentary law.

Leaders' Conferences. In addition to the experience in the local churches, special conferences should be arranged for church officers and other leaders, both men and women, where they can gather for a period of from five to ten days and receive definite instruction regarding their duties and responsibilities. At such times, notably the Pastoral Epistles and the Book of Acts should be the subject of careful study, in order that each one may realize his position and his responsibility as an officer of the church. As these leaders come to realize their duties from a Scriptural basis, they will also learn the necessity of studying the Word, of becoming familiar with the Person and the leadership of the Holy Spirit and the place of prayer in their own lives and that of the church. At these conferences there should also be special instruction in matters of organization, of leading in prayer in public services and in personal work as well as in the formal presentation or preaching of the gospel; standards of Christian living and the way to pass on those standards to the believers and members of the churches should also be taught. There should be periods for the discussion of specific problems which may have arisen in some of their churches, how they have met the difficulties. At such times full and frank discussions as to the relationship between the missionary and the national church and its officers, if carried on in the right way, will do much to preserve that cordial relationship of confidence and trust between the foreign missionary and his fellow workers, which is absolutely necessary if the work is to go ahead. Here again, humility will have to be exercised continually on the part of the missionary, and he must exhibit his willingness to be criticized and to give reasons for his actions and his attitudes. At best he is a "foreigner" and will be always regarded as such, and therefore must be prepared often to be misunderstood by even his closest associates. Frankness and humility must be habitually exercised in order to maintain the spirit of co-operation necessary for the growth of the work.

METHODS OF ORGANIZATION

With the formation of each group of new believers, church organization comes into being. It should therefore be emphasized again that before any new work is opened, the whole question of church organization should be carefully thought through, so that just as soon as Christians have been won and groups formed there will be a definite plan brought into action immediately. This plan should look forward to placing the responsibility upon the local leaders from the opening days. A strong lay-leadership can only be brought into being through careful and systematic training. In many mission fields, notably Korea and parts of China, the local short-term Bible institutes have proved to be of great use for this work. In these, promising young men are brought in for from one to two months, and young women for perhaps two and a half months or longer, to receive a carefully planned course of Bible study. As this is carried on once a year, young men especially are prepared to begin to take part in conducting worship and in bearing the burden of the responsibility of leadership in their local churches, with a well-rounded spiritual background as a basis.

As the church develops and the need grows, teacher-training institutes, both for teachers in Sunday schools and in extension Sunday schools will be carried on; Bible conferences will be planned and finally one of the Bible institutes should be expanded and developed into a theological seminary that will give the necessary specialized training for those who are called into the definite pastorate.

In Korea, in line with the spirit of self-support, which has formed one of the outstanding characteristics of much of the mission work there from the beginning, even in connection with these short-term Bible institutes and also the theological seminary, the policy has always been maintained that the expenses of the students are to be borne not by the mission but by the students themselves, or in many cases by the churches from which the students come. The missions at first usually provided the Bible institute buildings in which the classes were conducted and dormitories were erected, but with the growth of the work the Korean church established other Bible institutes, putting up the necessary buildings and carrying on the instruction with or without the help of missionaries. The duty of keeping the rooms clean and the buying and preparation of the food was left wholly to the students themselves. In most mission fields, to invite students, and especially young Christians, to come in and study at the expense of either the mission or the missionary, is an unfortunate, if not dangerous, practice. Experience has often shown that people may easily be attracted to come and study with unworthy motives, and money spent in that way has proved to be a very poor investment with no permanent spiritual returns.

QUESTIONS FOR DISCUSSION

1. Discuss the work and the value of a personal helper or secretary from the point of view of (1) the missionary, and (2) the church.
2. Discuss the possibilities of training church leaders through

two ways mentioned in this chapter. Should one be considered more important than the other? Are both necessary?

3. Why is it important to have thought through the whole plan for church organization before beginning the work?

4. Is there an argument for allowing the church to develop as it wants to?

5. Discuss the plan for training conferences and short-term Bible institutes and name what you would consider satisfactory courses for each.

CHAPTER X

SELF-GOVERNMENT

THE GREAT importance of taking the nationals in from the very beginning as advisers in all forms of the work is nowhere more true than in the matter of self-government. Having an intimate knowledge of the psychology and habits of thought of their own people, they will of necessity be the deciding factor in many questions, especially those in regard to discipline, and standards of Christian living. In this connection it is of importance to remember that in heathen countries every phase of life is shot through with superstition and ancient customs. Only a national, therefore, thoroughly familiar with them, is able to distinguish between superstition and customs which have no particular religious significance.

In the opening stages of the work the foreign missionary must occupy the place of leadership, but he should relinquish it as soon as nationals are ready to take it over! In certain places, however, the missionary has been slow to relinquish it, and after years or even decades of work, there is still a tendency to seek to dominate the life and the decisions of the church. In these cases it is easy to see that real self-government has scarcely begun. Especially in these days of acute nationalistic feeling and racial self-consciousness in almost every country, it should be clearly recognized in every land that the missionaries must increasingly be ready to occupy a secondary place, at least officially, in the government of the churches, which should rightly be in the hands of their own people. There have been instances wherein missionaries have held on to authority too long, causing tension and anti-foreign feeling, so that when the break finally came and the transfer of authority made, for some time the missionaries have been forced to take a subordinate position in the work of the church. As tension lessened, however, they were invited back again and into cordial relationship with those who at one time regarded the missionaries' presence and advice as unwanted and who were undeniably frank in the expression of their opinion and sentiment.

Form of Church Organization

The form of church organization is important, but I will make only two comments:

Should be Adapted to Present Conditions. The forms of church organization as we now know them in our land are the results of decades, if not centuries, of development and progress. In most cases they are far removed from the simpler forms that existed during the Apostolic age. Just because a certain form of church organization has proved successful in America or in the Western world is no proof that it is needed in the Orient or in lands where the church is still in its infant state. The pioneer missionaries, therefore, upon whom will fall the responsibility of planning the organization of a new church, should be prepared to adapt it to the conditions and needs of the people at that particular area, knowing that it can always be modified and doubtless will change as the nationals are ready to make it better adapted to their own needs. At the time of the formation of the Korean Presbyterian Church and the working out of its Constitution, careful studies were made of the forms of Presbyterian government in other mission fields and in Western lands, and a form was drawn up containing the more desirable features. As the work developed, additions were made, including the recognition of one or two new grades of church officers. These have proved very satisfactory and have made great contributions to the progress of the church.

Advantages of Presbyterian over Congregational Form of Government. While doubtless many, both in the homelands and on the mission fields, will insist that the Congregational form of government is the Scriptural form and the one best fitted for progress, my own experience has convinced me that especially in the beginning of a new church, the Presbyterian form is preferable. The practical advantages are seen when it is remembered that the groups of believers, which are usually small, form a very small minority in comparison with the great heathen population all about them and they are under tremendous pressure from the influence of centuries of heathenism and superstitious customs. In view of this, then, uniform policies and standards are a source of great moral strength, and the knowledge that the other groups in that territory are maintaining the same standards while meeting similar opposition will be a source of real strength and encouragement. In mission fields a strong system of church discipline is very helpful, both in establishing and in maintaining high standards of Christian living. When these matters are left in the hands of the individual congregations, no uniform policy is likely to result, and where local pressure is strong, the particular group of believers may be led to compromise and thereby weaken their testimony before the pagan world as well as weaken their own convictions. The same thing applies when it comes to the needed discipline of men of high social or official position who have failed to live up to the standards set by the church. Here also if left to the local congregation, the prestige of the individual concerned might prevent the church from taking the required action. When a group of churches together, or a presbytery, bears the responsibility, the matter can be handled much more efficiently.

Another way in which this Presbyterian form of government is found helpful is in the care of newly-organized groups of believers. Where an individual church might feel unable to assume the entire responsibility for some recently-formed groups of believers, or of establishing others in unevangelized territories, the presbytery can take action, definitely committing certain areas to special churches or groups of churches. In this way it is possible for a number of churches by combining their means and efforts and unaided by supervision, to make effective provision for new work.

CHURCH OFFICERS

For centuries in the Orient there has been a great respect for a title, and once a man is elected to do an office in the church, he may carry that title for life. This often means a greater desire for the prestige involved.

Elders. The name and office of elder come naturally in the Orient, where the outstanding men of intelligence and of age are known as the "elders" to whom deference is due and who are naturally regarded as the leaders in the community. As a general thing, therefore, the office of elder or deacon often carries with it a far greater responsibility and dignity than is usual in the United States. It is a common practice for the elders to sit on the platform with the minister and to take an active part in the worship service. In many places, especially where the minister is in charge of more than one church, it is the regular practice for the elders or deacons to lead the Sunday evening or mid-week prayer meeting services, and they can always be called on for such purposes in an emergency. The church session, composed of the pastor and the elders of a congregation, is often called on to adjust quarrels and misunderstandings between Christians. In one of the northern towns of Korea, in which over half of the population of 15,000 are church members, the Japanese chief of police testified that during the ten years he was in residence there, there was never a case brought to him for adjustment between two Christians. All such disagreements were as a matter of course taken before the sessions of the local churches.

"Preparatory Elders." This is an office which was established by the missionaries in the early days in Korea. As new Christian groups were being formed, the missionary appointed one of the older and more mature Christians to this office, giving him for the time being the leadership of the church. It was generally understood to be an office looking forward to eldership; and when the number of members of any one church became sufficiently large to warrant an election, it was a usual thing for the man who had been acting as "preparatory elder" to be elected to the eldership. In this way a standard was set and a precedent was made whereby the right kind of man for this important office could be prepared in advance by the missionary or national pastor in charge.

Deacons. As in other countries, in Korea also, the deacons are men and women elected by the congregation, and are in charge of the finances of the church. They take care of the offerings and have a vital responsibility concerning all church expenses and the use to which the funds are put. The men very often are called upon to lead the services and to go out in the nearby villages on preaching tours and to conduct family worship and other services in the homes of Christians.

Exhorters. This office is held by both men and women and has been found to be a very useful addition to church organization. In the larger churches the church parish is divided into a certain number of districts which usually contain between five and fifteen Christian families, and one man and one woman exhorter are appointed in each of these districts, by the session. It is the duty of these people to keep in touch with each one of the families in the district and to report to the pastor any cases of sickness or of sorrow, or of needed discipline. Often district prayer meetings are held in the homes, and are led by the church officers or by the exhorters themselves. Once a month a meeting is held with the pastor, at which time a report is given from each district. In countries where telephones do not exist, this office is most useful in keeping the pastor in touch with the needs and the conditions of the homes represented in his church.

Bible Women. These women are supported by the church, who pays them a salary commensurate with their needs, sometimes in money, sometimes in grain. They very often accompany the pastor as he makes his calls, especially when he is visiting the women of his congregation, when it would be unwise for a man to do so alone. They also visit the sick and spend a good deal of time visiting in non-Christian homes, presenting the gospel and doing all they can to win the affection and confidence of the people in order to lead them out to the church. These women are usually chosen from among the widows of mature faith and many have had Bible institute training. They have made a tremendous contribution to the growth of the churches.

STANDARDS OF ADMISSION

The standards of admission into full church membership must be carefully and prayerfully thought through, so that a decision can be reached which will be for the entire area. In Korea, admission into the full membership of the church is not too easy. After a person has made a public profession of faith he is enrolled as "one who desires to enter" and places himself under instruction. After not less than six months he comes before the session and is questioned as to his family, his faith, and his Christian experience. The regularity of his attendance at the services of the church, both on Sunday and at prayer meeting is also noted and careful account must be given for any absences when sickness is not the reason. When he shows evidences of really understanding what faith in the Lord is and what it means in his own personal life, he is enrolled as a catechumen or inquirer. At a public service he is asked questions before the congregation as to his personal faith and experience, and takes vows of obedience and loyalty to the Lord. Not less than six months later he is eligible to be examined for baptism, provided that his conduct in the meantime has been in accordance with the recognized Christian standards. This will include not opening his shop on Sunday or working in his fields on the Lord's Day. It will also mean that he has not himself married or allowed his children to marry unbelievers during that time. After examination again, by the vote of the session he is admitted into the church by baptism. In this second examination various matters are required of him, which are worthy of note: (1) His ability to read; the Korean alphabet being the simplest in the world, there is no excuse for a person who is in earnest for not learning to read the Word of God; and so with the exception of people who are over fifty, it is generally understood that people who are unable to read are not ready for baptism. (2) His spiritual intelligence and experience are carefully looked into. This will include an understanding of what salvation is, how it is obtained, and what it involves. It means an understanding also of the meaning of the sacraments of the Lord's Supper and of baptism; it includes a knowledge of the Ten Commandments, the Lord's Prayer, and the Apostles' Creed. It means an understanding of some of the parables and some of the miracles and the main facts of the Lord's life. (3) A strict observance of the Lord's Day is considered absolutely necessary, and if a man has failed in his attendance at church except for matters of sickness, his baptism is usually deferred until the next quarter. (4) The use of alcohol must be entirely given up before baptism can be administered. (5) Ancestral worship with all its practices must be laid aside. (6) Personal work on the part of each individual believer has always been regarded in Korea as a "must" and there has been a strong feeling that unless a person has sufficient faith and earnestness to speak to others about the Lord, there is every reason to doubt the reality and sincerity of his faith. This emphasis on personal work on the part of all members has been one of the great secrets of the rapid growth of the church in Korea, which after a little over fifty years possessed a constituency of half a million.

STANDARDS OF CHRISTIAN LIVING

It is difficult for us who are living in a so-called Christian land, where the Gospel has been a matter of common knowledge for so long, to appreciate the difficulties of setting Christian standards. In I Corinthians 4:16 the Apostle Paul writes, "I beseech you therefore, be ye imitators of me," and again in Philippians 3:17, "Brethren, be ye imitators together of me, and mark them that so walk even as ye have us for an ensample," and again in I Thessalonians 1:6, "And ye became imitators of us, and of the Lord." In Paul's day there had not yet grown up the recognized standards of Christian living, and therefore when men and women came out of stark paganism and superstition and wanted to know what it meant to live as a Christian, all Paul could say was, "Be ye imitators of me or of us." A similar problem faces the missionary in the early days of the proclamation of the gospel in a heathen country, and one of the first steps he has to take, together with the recognized leaders of the national church, is the establishment of standards of Christian living, especially as they apply to the customs of that land. Among these the following will be included.

Establishing Christian Homes. The word "home" has many hallowed and tender associations which cluster around it for us. In a heathen country, however, such associations are almost entirely unknown, and in many lands where the influence of the gospel has not been felt, the word "home" is practically untranslatable. This is readily understandable when it is remembered that in the average "heathen" home, love between husband and wife, as we have come to know it, is absolutely unknown; it is neither expected nor desired. In most Oriental countries when the boys are married, they do not set up housekeeping and establish their own homes, but their wives are brought in under the parental roof. In such cases, if the young man should show undue fondness for his wife, it would easily result in great jealousy on the part of his mother (in a non-Christian home), and it is a commonly accepted fact that it is far better for the welfare of the entire family when such an attitude does not develop. As a rule, in many countries the marriage arrangements are all made by a "middle man" or agent, at the request of the parents; and it has been the usual custom for the bride and groom not to be allowed even to see each other, much less speak, until after the wedding ceremony has been completed.

I can remember a conversation with a young man who became my secretary. After working with me for some months, I asked him whether or not he had family prayers in his home. He said, "Yes," and then went on to tell me his experience. He said, "When I was a boy in my father's home, of course we had family prayers, and when my father was not present, I as the eldest son took them. At that time all the members of my rather large family and our servants and the workers on the farm came in, and we had prayers together, and I thought nothing of it; but when I came to work for you and brought my wife and children and we were living by ourselves in a home, I found it very different. According to Korean custom, a young husband and wife never sit down and talk together, and I found it exceedingly embarrassing to ask my wife to come and sit with me in the same room and read the Bible and sing hymns. I tried it several times but could not muster up courage, so finally one morning I asked the children to come in and we would sing some hymns, and then my wife took the hint and she came in, too, and since then we have had no trouble!"

At the times of the Bible conferences we often used to have the elders and deacons and church leaders come to our home for meals. More than once they have stopped in the midst of a meal and talked among themselves, saying, "Well, one of these days we Koreans will have to come to this and learn to sit down around the same table with our wives and our children. It will be rather embarrassing but when we get used to it, it will be a good thing!"

Similarly, in those lands where ancestor worship and filial piety have long held sway, the relationship between father and son is something difficult for us to realize. Christian fathers have often asked me to speak to their sons to find out what the boys were thinking, inasmuch as they, as their fathers, could never get down together on the same mat with their sons and have a heart-to-heart talk. This was from men who were elders, but had not yet caught the vision of what the relationships in a real Christian home can be, and particularly the relationship of father and son as it should be in the Lord.

Under the establishing of Christian homes will come not only instruction concerning the relationships between husbands and wives and parents and children, as contained in Ephesians 5 and 6, Colossians 3 and 4, I Peter 3, and similar passages, but also instruction in the feeding and care of babies, the training of children, elementary hygiene and information concerning diet. The need for every one of these is desperate in nearly all pagan lands.

Christian Marriages. This subject has already been referred to in connection with the widespread rule that believers are permitted to marry only believers. In practically all mission fields, it is the church law that Christian girls shall marry only Christian men, although in some countries Christian men are allowed to marry non-Christian girls, with the expectation that it will mean the conversion of their wives. This, however, does not always work out and many of the young men who are married to non-Christian women have suffered years of sorrow and heartache and on some occasions have been pulled down themselves by their wives, who have refused to accept the gospel. In regard to the arrangement of Christian marriages, the question of age is one which the church very often has to settle, especially in those countries where the government has made no age limit. In some lands the children mature much more rapidly than in the West, and without time for education as we know it, they are married off at a very much younger age, sometimes as early as ten or twelve. In such lands it is necessary for the church to decide on the earliest age at which children of Christians may be married, or even engaged. In such countries marriage is a matter of alliance between families rather than between individuals, and therefore the persons most concerned usually have little opportunity to express their own personal preferences or make their own decisions. In Christian weddings the rule has usually been established that if they so desire, the young people concerned may at least have an opportunity of seeing each other before their engagement is formally ratified.

In many lands also the question of concubinage or the taking of secondary wives is a very vital problem. The treatment of this question will differ in different lands on account of the varying circumstances. In some places the wives taken later are considered on a par with the first wives, whereas in the Orient, only the first wife has any legal standing and the rest are concubines. The church has to rule in regard to these matters as to whether a man has a right to be baptized while possessing more than one wife, and the same with a woman, whether she has any right to be baptized while in the position of a concubine or secondary wife. In Korea the church has felt very strongly that only when all such relationships have been definitely and finally dissolved is a person ready to be baptized and become a full member of the church. It is very essential that a Christian marriage ceremony be carefully worked out so that it will not only make clear the sanctity of the relationship between husband and wife in God's sight but will be a real testimony before the non-Christians present. Christian standards for the entertainment of guests at such ceremonies must also be settled so that the entire occasion shall be a definite gospel witness. As has been said before, in nearly all of these questions the foreign missionary alone cannot possibly make the wise decision and it must be made in conference with the Christian nationals who thoroughly understand the background.

Christian Funerals. In heathen countries weddings and

funerals are two great social occasions, and often the money spent for such ceremonies is out of all proportion to the income of the families concerned. The Christians therefore have had to decide on standards governing these matters. In Korea many of the churches have formed their own burial societies, and it is understood that when any member of the church dies, each of the families will send at least one representative and a certain number of candles and paper, which are used not in any sense as a religious element but are used by the household during the days in which the body is lying in state. The churches also have found it advisable, if not necessary, to build their own biers so as to give more of a Christian appearance to the ceremony. A very strong stand is taken against the serving of liquor, which is the chief attraction in heathen burials. The mourning customs in every country vary greatly, but anything which savors of superstitious significance must be carefully removed from the ceremony in order that the funerals themselves may be testimonies to the power of the gospel and to the faith for which the church stands.

Food Offered to Idols. A very acute question in the early church, referred to by the Apostle Paul in several of his letters, was the matter of Christians eating food which had been offered to idols. The same thing is a very live question today in many foreign mission fields, especially in those in which ancestral worship is observed and ancestral sacrifices are made. The standards set down by the Apostle Paul are eminently practicable as the same questions are faced today, and when the missionaries are ready to sit down with the national Christians and discuss all these questions from the Scriptural standpoint and prepare to settle them on a Scriptural basis, there need be no uncertainty as to what stand should be taken.

The Exercise of Discipline by the Church. Church discipline, through its official representatives, is referred to in a number of the New Testament Epistles and was evidently a function of the Apostolic Church. In mission fields, where conditions very often closely approximate those which were common to the early church, church discipline, when exercised according to Scriptural principles, has proved to be very beneficial to the spiritual life of the members and an effective aid also in maintaining the standards of Christian living. Inasmuch as it is the church bodies which set the standards in regard to admission to membership and the standards of Christian living, it must again be the church which sets the rules for the discipline and the governing of the membership. It will also be the church that exercises that discipline in accordance with the rules it has made. As a general thing the nationals are far more severe in discipline than most foreign missionaries either care or dare to be. Certainly when the nationals make the decision it is done in a way that causes no anti-foreign feelings against the missionary and nearly always makes for a very deep-rooted respect for the laws of the church and for the stand which it has taken. I remember one occasion in the early days in Korea when one of the Korean ministers was found guilty of having engaged his son to be married a few weeks before the boy had reached the age limit decided upon by the church. At the meeting of the presbytery the matter was taken up in the appropriate committee and then reported back to the presbytery. After considerable discussion the motion was made and passed that the minister guilty of engaging his son a few weeks too early was forbidden to preach in his pulpit for six months. He was not deprived of his church and was permitted to sit on the platform at the services, but was not allowed to lead in any of the services. It is needless to say that that stern discipline was a severe warning and no other minister in the following years was guilty of making the same mistake.

Discipline to be effective must be administered with a full knowledge of the psychology and background of the person who is receiving it, in order that it may be well understood as to what effect it is going to have upon those most deeply concerned. It is the nationals themselves who understand this best and therefore they must be the ones to determine the standards and where possible to administer the discipline.

In the Korean Church, discipline is administered in several degrees. In milder cases a summons to appear before the local church session and a rebuke from that body has proved sufficient, together with a warning that a more severe action will be taken if the error is repeated. In cases where more decisive action is deemed advisable, on action of the session, the names of the guilty members are read out before the congregation together with a brief statement of their sins, such as failure to observe the Lord's Day, their marriage or the marriage of their children to non-Christians, or taking part in ancestral sacrifices. As a penalty they may be debarred from the Lord's table for at least six months and until they had shown true repentance and a sincere return to the Lord. If they show no apparent desire to return to the faith and to live up to the required standards, after the lapse of one or two years, the names are often erased from the church roll.

Such strict exercise of discipline may at first sight seem to savor largely of legalism; but in young churches when it is carried out, it makes for a strong and clear-cut witness before the heathen population and makes a profound impression as to the necessity for being sincere in one's profession of faith in Jesus Christ and for living consistent with the profession.

QUESTIONS FOR DISCUSSION

1. Discuss the factors to be considered in judging the form of church government that will be best adapted to the needs of the people.
2. What are the two classes of church officers mentioned in the New Testament? List their qualifications as recorded there and discuss the practicability of insisting on the same basis today in the mission field.
3. What consideration should be given to the appointment or election of additional grades of church officers for the development of the church?
4. Discuss what you regard as necessary standards of admittance to full church membership, listing what should be required of prospective members.
5. How soon after profession of faith has been made should a person be considered for baptism? Outline a course of instruction to be given to such.
6. Discuss what you would consider essential factors in:
   A Christian home
   A Christian wedding ceremony
   A Christian funeral service
7. What would you consider the Scriptural and practical attitude in regard to eating food offered to idols or in ancestral sacrifices?
8. Discuss the value of exercising church discipline and outline how it should be administered and for what offenses.

CHAPTER XI

SELF-PROPAGATION

T HE MORE a church realizes its responsibility and exercises its right to govern itself, the more rapidly will it become interested in the work of self-propagation and in the development of its own spiritual life and influence throughout the community.

AIM—"EVERY CHRISTIAN AN ACTIVE WITNESS"

The well-known motto, "Saved to serve," might well be changed to "Saved to Save." From the start every possible emphasis should be placed upon the personal responsibility of all believers, as soon as they are sure of their salvation, to go out to tell others what the Lord has meant to them. This was one of the great secrets of the growth of the early church (Acts 8:4-12; 11:19; 15:35). In Korea it has been well understood that unless a person has sufficient faith and earnestness to go out to do personal work, he is not ready to be baptized nor prepared to take on the full responsibility of church membership. Volumes could be filled with interesting stories of the results of the personal work done in Korea and many other mission fields by national pastors and laymen whose hearts have been kindled with a love for their Lord and have been burdened by the lost condition of the people around them.

Pastor Kang, a man well-versed in the Chinese classics and a sound Christian, was arrested and imprisoned for two years at the time of the Independence Movement in 1919. I was almost the first foreigner to gain admission to visit him while he was in jail. I saw him engaged in making cigarette boxes in a large cell with seventy other prisoners. After his release his testimony was much as follows: "I had always prayed that the Lord would give me the privilege of proclaiming the gospel of Jesus Christ in the thirteen provinces of our country, and I had looked forward to doing so some day. But the Lord knew better; perhaps He thought I was getting too old to visit all thirteen provinces; so instead, He put me in the West Gate Jail in Seoul, and brought men from the thirteen provinces to me!"

During the two years of his imprisonment Pastor Kang led ninety-seven of his fellow-prisoners to faith in Christ. Among them he carefully examined and enrolled a number as catechumens or inquirers and from among them he later baptized seven or eight whom he felt had proved their fitness for the step. When those men left the prison to return to their homes, they carried with them letters of dismissal from the Presbyterian Church in the West Gate Jail of Seoul! Needless to say, neither the Japanese nor the Korean jailers had any knowledge of the existence of any such church nor of the effective evangelism which was being carried on. Similar instances could be duplicated many times.

Organized Personal Evangelism

In addition to instruction that personal evangelism should be regarded as an individual responsibility and a normal activity on the part of every Christian, a great stimulus and encouragement can be given to such work by definitely organizing the church members along several lines.

Tract Distribution. The distribution of tracts is always one of the most effective as well as one of the easiest ways to start off new believers in the discharge of their responsibility. Systematic tract distribution on market days and throughout villages by bands of Christians has been productive of excellent results, not only for the receivers but also for the givers. In Korea as a part of practically every Bible conference, whether large or small, those who attended were always sent out each afternoon to systematically cover all the neighboring villages, giving out the tracts and, where possible, adding a word of personal testimony and extending an urgent invitation to attend the evening meetings to learn of the "doctrine."

"Days of Preaching." In the early days a very effective way of promoting personal evangelism was to give opportunities for the people in the various churches to volunteer to spend a specified number of days in tract distribution and personal work. When the missionary or pastor in charge visited a church in the fall season, during one of the services he would ask each one to raise his hand and announce the number of days he would pledge himself to engage in this work during the winter months when work on the farms was slack. Both men and women would offer to give from five to thirty days each; thus a small congregation might easily pledge several months.

Individuals to Be Prayed for and Evangelized. Another plan sometimes used has been for the pastor to request each member of the church to write on a piece of paper the names of three persons for whom he or she would himself promise to pray for and with whom he would guarantee to spend time in personal evangelism. The names were then handed to the pastor, who would record them in a book, and after a period of from six to nine months the names would be checked and reports given on how many of those had been won to faith in the Lord.

The church buildings are rarely locked but are kept open for any who desire to go in to pray. The average home consists of two rooms about eight feet square and a kitchen, which is largely exposed to the open air; so there is little chance for privacy for Christians in a home where there are also non-Christians. In one city church of about 250 members, the pastor told me that an average of about twenty-five people came each morning before daybreak for prayer. Many of them were women praying for their non-Christian husbands. At times the whole church would spend an entire night in prayer on behalf of a revival and for the non-Christian friends and relatives. The Lord never fails to honor such earnestness.

Provision for Immigrants. In the early days of Korean migration into Manchuria when Korean settlers were moving in large numbers in order to escape the high taxation and oppression of the Japanese Government, the churches in the Korean settlements already established in Manchuria would set aside large supplies of grain in order to feed these immigrants as they came in during the cold winter months. The churches along the main roads of travel were used as hostels and the newcomers would be allowed to sleep in them and were fed for days or weeks until they had found a place in which to settle. By this practical form of Christian hospitality the hearts of many were won and great numbers of them found the Lord as a result of this generous provision by the Christians.

ORGANIZED CHURCH EVANGELISM

As personal evangelism yields larger results when organized, so also does the evangelistic work of the church as a whole bring greater increases when it is carefully organized. This should be started early in the life of the church.

Missionary Societies. In the work in Korea every church

had its women's missionary society, which met once or twice each month. It was the custom always to receive an offering made in grain, as so few of the women ever had any money pass through their hands. They would set aside a spoonful or two of grain from each meal and put it into a little bag to keep for the use of the church; much of this was put aside for the missionary society. In this way in the course of a few months, even in the small churches, several bushels of grain would be received. Some trained Bible women from elsewhere, or possibly one of the better educated women of that church, was invited to go out to some unevangelized village and spend a month or more doing personal work among the women, using the grain as her support during that time. In this way practically every church, no matter how small, was carrying on a forward evangelistic program by the women among the women of its area.

Home Missionary Societies. In addition to the work carried on by the women of each church, each individual church itself made a contribution each year to the home missionary society of the presbytery or conference. This money was used in supporting one or more men, or sometimes women, while they spent their time in unevangelized villages, preaching the gospel and planting new groups and churches.

Christian Families "Settled" in Unevangelized Villages. In some areas, in place of sending a man in to do evangelistic work for several months in a village, it was found to be more effective to use the money that would otherwise be spent for his support during that time, to buy a field or a house. This the interested church or group of churches would put at the disposal of a Christian man who would move there with his family and farm or keep a store, with the understanding that he would conduct family worship in his own home regularly, and as soon as they were settled would hold services on Sunday, inviting the neighbors in. Through that means it often proved possible to establish a little group within a year and on a self-supporting basis.

Home and Foreign Mission Boards. Shortly after the Korean Presbyterian Church was organized as a national church about fifty years ago, it elected its Board of Foreign Missions, and undertook the support of an ordained pastor to go down to the Island of Quelpart, off the south coast, to open evangelistic work there. A few years later they began work in China, and for thirty-five years had been supporting three ordained pastors and their wives as foreign missionaries in the Province of Shantung, until the work was shut down by World War II. The funds for the support of these men were raised by special offerings made on Thanksgiving Day. Thanksgiving Day celebration was usually preceded by a week of special prayer and very often Bible study, at the close of which an offering was taken for the cause of foreign missions. Later a similar offering on Easter Sunday was used for the Board of Home Missions, which supported some fourteen or twenty workers, including both ordained pastors and women at work among the Koreans in Japan proper, in Shanghai, and in Manchuria.

Evangelistic Campaigns. Evangelistic campaigns conducted for the most part by Korean pastors have been highly successful. Churches have been warmed and revitalized as whole congregations have gone out during the afternoons for tract distribution, personal work, and to gather in large numbers of unbelievers for the great public evening services.

Evangelistic Work by Students. In some of the boys' academies and colleges Christian students were sent out each Sunday to organize extension Sunday schools and to preach in nearby country villages. During vacations a number of evangelistic teams were sent out, supported by offerings made by the faculty and students, visiting the various provinces, and returned reporting thousands of professed conversions. When the young men of the church become interested to the point where they are willing to go out in evangelistic campaigns, they are used by the Holy Spirit in a wonderful way to the arousing and awakening of fresh interest. When they have gone through a spiritual experience which has caused a transformation in their lives and has set them on fire with a new patriotic fervor and love for their own countrymen, they are willing to endure great hardships and go out into the very roughest and wildest parts of the country to present the gospel to those who are still living in ignorance and sin.

Foreign Missionaries in Unevangelized Villages. In order to promote evangelistic efforts, the foreign missionary himself must be ready to set the example and the lead. When missionaries become so tied down with ministering to the organized churches and the unorganized groups of believers that they have no time to spend in reaching out to unevangelized districts, the whole evangelistic interest of the church may suffer. It is a very healthy rule for each missionary to spend at least from two weeks to a month each year in unevangelized villages, together with a few national Christians, in order to encourage and train others to do that essential work. It means personal sacrifices and discomfort and other more attractive work will have to be put aside for the time being. The results, however, both in the lives of those who preach and of those who are reached more than compensate for any apparent losses.

Nothing Can Take the Place of Personal Influence. Experience both in this country and elsewhere has shown that the most effective means of building up a church is through the personal work of its members. Evangelistic campaigns and similar efforts have a very real place, but when it comes to the permanent and steady growth of a church, it is the work by the members that counts most. More than once at gatherings of men's Bible conferences I have asked the men how they came to make the decision to believe. I would ask those who believed as a result of reading a tract to raise their hands; perhaps three or four or at most half a dozen would do so; then, I would ask how many came to believe through reading the New Testament, but I rarely got any hands at all; I then asked how many decided to believe as a result of dropping in at a church service and hearing something said by the minister which touched their heart, but again there were rarely any hands shown. However, when I asked how many had come to believe as a result of the personal efforts of their friends or the believing members of their family, then a great number went up. My final question was this, "How many of you had decided to believe as the result of watching the lives of the Christians in your neighborhood, and realizing that they possessed a peace and a power and a joy which you did not have and which you wanted?" This brought the largest number of all.

For that reason, one of the essentials—as has already been mentioned—is the insisting on a high standard of Christian living that will from the beginning set apart the lives of the Christians from the lives of those outside the church; so that the world may know that when a man takes a stand for the Lord, it is going to mean a transformation of his life, of his way of living, of his motives, and of his whole personality. Nothing can equal that for awakening in others the desire and then the will to believe.

QUESTIONS FOR DISCUSSION

1. Discuss the importance of impressing every church member with his privilege and responsibility of witnessing to others; and outline means whereby this impression may be made.
2. Discuss the various forms of organized personal evangelism mentioned, emphasizing those plans which seem to be the most practical in the specific mission field in which you are interested.
3. Discuss what you think can be done the most effectively to promote giving by new Christians, both of their means and of their time, in the interests of evangelizing nearby territories.
4. How prominent a part should a foreign missionary take in personal evangelism and in organized evangelistic campaigns in order to stimulate the national Christians to engage in such work?

Chapter XII

SELF-SUPPORT

THE THIRD outstanding essential of an indigenous church is self-support. Self-support has been put last, because as a rule it has proved to be one of the most difficult things to obtain and, under ordinary circumstances, self-support is not gained until self-government has been at least partially, if not wholly, put into effect. Until a man realizes that the church is his, and his to have a voice in its organization and procedure, he is not going to be too much interested in paying for its support and meeting the expenses of upkeep and of further expansion.

Basic Principles

As this matter of self-support is considered, a few basic principles should be constantly kept in mind.

Nationals' Reluctance to Raise Money if Foreign Missionaries Will Supply It. In most mission fields the homes of missionaries are much more comfortable and their scale of living is far higher than that of the common people among whom they work. This is not said in any spirit of criticism of the missionaries, for their health and the effectiveness of their work depends in a large measure upon the maintenance of those standards of living. Often when I was in Korea, country people would come in and ask to look over our house, and as they saw the rugs and the pictures and the books, they would say, "Will heaven be any nicer than this?" From their point of view, therefore, it is only natural to think it far easier for a foreign missionary, if he so desires, to secure a hundred dollars for church work than it would be for them in their poverty to raise one-tenth of that sum. Because of that, it is very easy for the nationals to speak of their poverty as the reason why they are unable to supply the needs of the work, and to plead for assistance from the foreign missionary. Too often missionaries have had their sympathies played upon by these pleas and have given far more than they had any right to do for the best interests of the people concerned.

Use of Foreign Funds Is a Barrier Between the People and

the Missionaries. I have had opportunities to check the truth of this statement in a number of missions and in several different mission lands and have found it almost always true that the anti-foreign feeling on the part of the Christians towards the missionaries is in exact proportion to the amount of foreign funds used. I shall never forget my first experience when this truth began to come home. It was at a meeting of the Korean General Assembly and one of the pastors was continually rising and making a number of speeches which were quite anti-foreign in their tenor and quite critical of foreign missionaries. After listening to a number of his harangues, I spoke to the missionary sitting next to me and said, "Who is this brother?" His reply was, "He is a pastor down in our territory, and he has received, I suppose, more help individually from the missionary in his district than any other one pastor in the country. The missionary has subsidized this man's salary from his own personal funds month by month, has furnished him a bicycle, has given him clothes for his children, and has helped by paying their tuition for them at the schools." In spite of this, or I believe I should say, because of the unwise generosity on the part of one missionary, the pastor in question had failed to appreciate the spirit in which the help had been given and had developed a grasping spirit and a lust for more help, which had embittered him against all foreigners, and he became for a number of years the outstanding anti-foreign member of the General Assembly.

In one of the annual publications of the Federated Christian Missions in Japan, many years ago, I well remember reading a symposium of the replies to a letter sent out by the writer to about a hundred leading Japanese Christians, both men and women, pastors and laymen. There were a number of pertinent questions asked in regard to relationship of missionaries and the Japanese church officials. One of the men said, "The most shameful experience I have had comes month by month when I receive my salary from a foreigner." These are but two examples, and many more could be stated if they were needed to show how the use of foreign funds easily causes friction and unrest between nationals and missionaries. It is easy to understand the reason for the development of this feeling. If foreign missionaries make a habit of paying the salaries of national workers, whether pastors or evangelists, it makes very little difference to the men in question whether the money comes from the private resources of the missionaries themselves or from the mission funds. In any event, they are receiving it from and through the missionaries. Under those conditions when one of them comes with the plea that he is unable to live on the salary he is receiving because of the high cost of living, or because of the increase of his family, and asks for more, the missionary may say, "I am sorry, my brother, but we have no more funds for that purpose." In the course of the discussion it is easy for the national pastor to say, "How much do you receive?" And on finding that the missionary's salary is from two to eight times as much as he has been receiving, it is very easy for him to say, "Well, supposing you received just $10.00 or $20.00 less a month and give that amount to me. Wouldn't that be fair? Are we not both brothers in Christ?" It places the missionary not only in an embarrassing position, but from the point of view of the national, in an almost unanswerable position, unless he can say that from the very beginning the funds for the salaries of the national pastors and workers have been raised by the churches themselves. Then, when a man finds that his salary is too low and complains to the missionary, the missionary is in a very strong position to go down to the church or churches responsible for that worker's support and plead with them on behalf of their own brother in Christ to do more than they have been doing, and usually with happy results.

The Origin of Funds Determines the Authority. As long as funds used in the church work come from or through the mission or missionaries, the nationals will never feel free to take a strong stand on the way in which those funds ought to be distributed. In other words, as long as the funds for a church come from a foreign source, that church or those churches will never properly assume the responsibility and function of being self-governing. In general, it is very difficult for a man on a salary supplied from foreign sources to express his opinion thoroughly and frankly. It is contrary to human psychology, and he is not in a position to think and to plan and to work to the utmost of his ability and independently for the further development of his own church.

In Korea, at the request of some friends in America who sent me some money for that purpose, I disobeyed the principle which I have been advocating thus far and sent out two or three evangelists for some months, supporting them on funds sent to me from friends in this country. As a result of their work, a number of new groups were started; but it was a matter of almost ten· years before any of those groups got on a strong basis of self-support, or self-government, or self-propagation. In one of those places, some years after the evangelist had left, an old man began talking to me and I found out that his son had been one of the first young men in the village to be interested in the gospel; but that on account of his drinking, he had given it up and had wandered back into sin. The old man, who was in no sense a Christian, said, "What a pity it was my son lost out and gave up the doctrine!"

I agreed with him, and then I said, "Why do you make that statement?"

He replied, "Oh, just think, if my son had continued to believe, well, by this time he might be drawing a salary and would be able to support me!"

In these words he made it plain to me that the fact that the evangelist who had preached the gospel in that village had been supported by foreign funds had made a deep impression on some. The evangelist had felt perfectly free to tell the people that fact, and when he was asked had freely explained both the source and the amount of the money he was receiving. This had quickly prompted his newfound friends to ask, "If I believe well enough, can I get a salary, too?" The reply to that question would naturally have to be in the affirmative. As a result, so far as that evangelist was concerned, the great bulk of those whom he had led to profess faith in Jesus Christ had been, whether unconsciously or otherwise, influenced with the hope that eventually through their faith they might be in a position to be on a regular salary and therefore better able to support their families. Nearly all of those who first professed to believe soon became discouraged and fell away.

In countries where religion always has been a matter of doing rather than believing, the relation of finances to workers has a peculiar significance. On one occasion in Tokyo I had the experience of meeting an influential banker who had just returned from a three months' trip to Korea where he had been sent by the Japanese Imperial Diet to investigate the work of the missionaries. He returned to Tokyo and was planning within two or three days to make his report to the Diet on the results of his visit. Fortunately I had the opportunity to meet with him and to ask and answer some questions. We conversed for an hour and a half on a variety of subjects. Among other interesting statements which he made was this one, "As a result of my investigation I understand that the Presbyterian missionaries in Korea receive their salaries in exact proportion to the number of converts which they make and report to their home boards; therefore, I am rather suspicious of the motives of the missionaries and of the truthfulness of their reports on the number of Korean Christians." I did my best to convince him he was thoroughly misinformed, but apparently he had gained his information through Japanese or Korean spies and was far more willing to believe them than he was to take my word. If a high Japanese government official would believe that about missionaries, it is not difficult to imagine what the country people would believe about national workers supported by mission funds!

Self-Support Is Essential in Order to Establish Strong Churches. For the last seventeen years of my life in Korea I was in one of the central provinces, which for centuries had been the most backward in every way of all the thirteen provinces. As a result of the evils of absentee landlordism, the people in the country—the majority of whom are tenants on the estates of the landed gentry—have long been downtrodden; and there is much illiteracy, poverty, and lack of initiative. On arriving at my station I found that because of those conditions, the missionaries in that particular district had been subsidizing the salaries of the unordained pastors in charge of circuits of the small and weaker groups. The missionaries, with mission funds usually, had undertaken to pay one-third of the total salary, the salary itself being very small. For a number of years after my arrival there we continued on that same system but the growth of the church was by no means encouraging and did not begin to keep up with the growth in the other parts of the country. On one occasion one of the Korean pastors from the North, who came down to accept a call as pastor of one of our local churches, told me frankly, "Pastor, you use far too much foreign money in this district."

I agreed with him and said, "How can we stop?"

"Well," he said, "why don't you turn the money over to the presbytery and ask them to distribute it?"

I replied that it was against our mission policy to do that but that I felt sure that we could ask the presbytery to appoint a committee to advise us and we would be very glad to follow the advice of our Korean brethren. This arrangement was made and the committee was appointed. The memory of that first committee meeting still remains with me very clearly. I explained to the committee, composed of three missionaries and three Korean pastors, that in view of the decision of our mission's policy, from now on within five years we would be forced to stop paying any money whatsoever in subsidies towards the salaries of these men and therefore it was necessary that either the churches to which they ministered, or the presbytery, somehow make greater efforts to see that sufficient money was raised. The Korean members on the committee then replied, "Now give us the names of the men, the amount of money you are paying them and we will give you advice as to what to do." So I started calling the names of the unordained pastors in charge of the circuits.

The first man's name was called—"What about him?"

"He is no good; he should be dropped."

I said, "But how can we do it? He has been on foreign pay now for nearly twenty years."

"Exactly, and that is the reason he is so poor. He is old, he is inefficient, he is out of date."

I said, "Well, do you mean that we should drop him at once?"

The reply was in favor of granting him six months' salary in advance, as "comfort money," and telling him to buy a field and go to farming or buy a house and do some other work or depend upon his sons; but to make it clear to him that his days of securing any salary from the missionaries were over. The motion was made to this effect and unanimously passed. Then we went down the list of the other men. In case after case the committee recommended that we should make a reduction in the monthly salary by two or three dollars each. When I inquired as to what steps would be taken to see that the churches increased their amount which they raised each month, their reply was that the presbytery would attend to that and that the Korean members of the committee would themselves visit the churches concerned and explain to the members that they were fully capable of raising more than they were then doing and that they must do so.

These recommendations were all passed by the presbytery at once with no opposition. Within three years after that plan was started, four-fifths of all the money had been taken care of. Shortly after this system had been put into operation one of the Korean ministers came to me one day and said, "Pastor, it is a matter of God's free grace that the money received from the mission for the salaries of these men has been cut down."

I agreed with him and said, "What makes you say so?"

"Well," he replied, "since that money has been practically done away with, the people in those churches have begun to realize that after all the churches are theirs and the responsibility is theirs to see that the churches are maintained properly and grow. As a result an entirely new spirit of initiative and of forward-looking planning has come about and things are really on the move."

I smiled with deep satisfaction as he said this. He saw my smile and added, "But remember, Pastor, it is also a matter of God's grace that it was we Koreans in the presbytery that decided to reduce those payments and not you missionaries. Had you foreigners taken the step, you would have been exceedingly unpopular and people would have said that you no longer had love for them. It might have hurt your influence tremendously."

Then again I smiled and said, "Amen."

I have proved that this principle holds in America also by personal experience with a small mission church in the state in which I am now living. Only as the people realize that the church is theirs and that they must meet all the expenses themselves is there going to be a real spirit of interest and of progress. Could every foreign missionary realize this before he or she is sent out to the foreign field, it would make a tremendous difference in the future development of the work and especially in the new work yet to be undertaken. What is true in regard to the salaries of the workers is equally true for the cost of church buildings.

In earlier years before I had learned my lesson properly, I was persuaded by enthusiastic evangelists to pay the cost of two Korean houses which were to be used by new groups as church buildings. In neither place was the financial sum large. In the first it was about seven dollars and in the second about forty. In each case an evangelist had gone in, a number of professed believers had been won, and the evangelist had come to me saying, "Pastor, there are so many people here, there is no house large enough to accommodate their meetings, and unless you do something for us they will all be lost." Because of his misguided enthusiasm I gave him the money and in each village a house was purchased which was then altered by the people themselves to make it suitable for holding services. In both cases, within three years the buildings were sold for what we could get for them. The people had been won to make a profession of faith in the belief that something was going to take place by which they could gain a great deal. They gained a house in which to meet, they gained a man to come and speak to them and teach them, all on foreign money; but when that money stopped their interest also stopped, and their faith collapsed. It was a bitter lesson but one which I was glad I had learned at that time before further money was wasted in the same way.

PRACTICES IN KOREA

The work in Korea which God has so greatly blessed has clearly shown that in the areas where the church has had the greatest progress, the following policies have contributed greatly to that success.

No Mission Funds for Pastors' Salaries. From the beginning of one mission, it has been an undeviating principle that no man would be ordained for the pastorate until one or possibly two churches together were in a position to undertake his full support, the minimum salary being set by each presbytery concerned.

No Mission Money for Church Properties. From the beginning no mission funds have been used for the purchase of church sites or the erection of church buildings. There have been a few exceptions to this for a particular reason. The mission allowed that in the case of one church building in each foreign mission station, up to one-third of the total cost might be defrayed from mission funds. This exception was made for the following reasons: It was always the custom to use the local church as the gathering place of the whole district for the great Bible conferences held once or twice each year. On that account the church inevitably had to be built considerably larger than would be necessary for the local congregation, and inasmuch as it was the presence of the missionaries residing in that place that caused the conference to be held there, they felt obligated to meet up to one-third of the expense of one building. This has meant that of the over three hundred churches erected in the area for which the mission was responsible, mission funds were used to meet one-third of the expenses involved in eight of them. This rule did not apply to Bible institute buildings, schools and hospitals, all of which were erected in the beginning with mission funds. As the work developed, plans were made by which joint Boards of Directors were formed, looking forward eventually to the taking over of the buildings and their support and maintenance by the Korean Church. In some cases, especially the Bible institutes and schools, that work was practically complete when the Second World War broke out.

No Mission Money for Evangelists' Salaries (that is, home missionaries). All the salaries of Korean workers carrying on active evangelistic work among their own people were raised by the Korean Church. That has been true from the beginning. On certain occasions, for a matter of a week or two, special mission funds set aside for that purpose, were used for an advance evangelistic program in which the expenses of those who accompanied the missionaries were paid by foreign funds, but no salaries of any kind were paid and no exceptions were made to this rule. In this way, from the start, the burden of the evangelistic work among the Korean people was placed squarely upon the infant church, which responded nobly and magnificently.

The Results. During the years 1934 to 1937, when conditions preceding the war became acute, the Korean Church in the district for which the Northern Presbyterian Mission was responsible, matched dollar for dollar all the money that came out from America for mission work, including furlough allowance, travel allowance, children's allowance, and all expenses of the missionaries together with the expenses of the property which was bought or erected by the mission. In 1937 a sum was contributed by a church with a baptized membership of about 120,000 equivalent to two and a half million days' wages. This is a remarkable manifestation of the successful way in which self-support has been carried through in that land where poverty abounds and the economic standards of living are far lower than those of Japan.

THE PROBLEM OF TRANSITION FROM THE OLD SYSTEM TO THE NEW

In a good many mission fields the work is still carried along more or less on the old line, that is to say, salaries, expenses, and buildings are paid from mission funds. A very pertinent question therefore arises, How shall the transition be made from the old system to the new? It is far more difficult to make a transition than it is to begin in a new field on the new basis.

The Foreign Missionaries Must First Be Convinced. When missionaries have been working along the old lines for several decades, it is very difficult for them to recognize that during that long period of time their work has been carried on on the wrong basis. In many cases it is the normal thing for such missionaries to regard the national Christians as their own spiritual children, for whom they must often think as well as pay the bills, and one of the most difficult parts of the problem is to get the missionaries themselves to be willing to admit that the changes must be made, even at the cost of misunderstanding and probable bitter criticism from the national Christians who have become accustomed to looking to foreign sources for the support of their churches.

The Nationals Will Be Unappreciative at First. To get the missionaries ready to make a change is not easy, and then when that change is put into practice, many difficult questions with the nationals are bound to arise. It is very much like getting children to walk, especially if they have become used to being carried around all the time by nurses. After the nationals have been used to having their salaries paid regularly by the missionaries, it is a very grave change for them to be taken over by their own countrymen. Difficulties of many kinds arise. The certainty of receiving their salary not only is questionable, but in most cases the salary itself will be considerably lower than when it was received from the foreign missionary. The time taken for the transition will depend largely upon the condition of the churches within the territory, the degree of development which has already taken place, and the financial condition of the members as a whole. As a general rule, it would be wise to draw up a five- or a ten-year plan, during which time there will be a gradual reduction of foreign funds. The plan should be clearly explained and then, regardless of circumstances, it should be carried out as proposed. In the Presbyterian work in Japan this was carried out on a ten-year basis and before the ten years were up the Japanese Christians in most cases were thoroughly convinced of the wisdom of the plan and were more than ready to meet their obligations. Previous to that time it was understood that only churches that were completely self-supporting were ready to go into the independent Church of Japan and those which were still dependent upon the mission for salaries remained outside the national church.

However, the Japanese government, shortly before the war, promulgated an edict forbidding the use of any foreign subsidies in any form of mission work so that churches and schools rapidly became completely independent and self-supporting. In one of the provinces in the far northwest of China a ten-year plan in one mission was adopted, but the Chinese reaction was so strong to it that long before the ten years had elapsed the Chinese church took over the entire responsibility of raising the funds and in many cases quickly made changes in the personnel of the men whom they supported. In a very short time the church in that section became indigenous and much more active and aggressive than it had ever been before.

QUESTIONS FOR DISCUSSION

1. Discuss the relationship between self-government, self-propagation, and self-support.
2. Name four basic principles concerning self-support and the use of foreign funds.
3. Explain the dangers of putting up foreign-style church buildings with foreign money.
4. Outline a plan for changing from the method of supporting national workers in whole or in part, where such has been the rule, to one of full self-support.

CHAPTER XIII

MISSION EDUCATIONAL WORK

T HE PROBLEM of mission education is a tremendous one. It is one concerning which volumes have already been written and doubtless many more will be written discussing its various phases and problems.

TWO VIEWS OF THE AIM OF MISSION EDUCATIONAL WORK

For a true evaluation of missionary education it is first of all necessary to have a carefully thought-out goal for the work itself. There are two widely differing opinions as to the purpose of missionary education. They are here briefly described.

1. *The Leavening of Society with Christian Ideals.* This view holds that the purpose of Christian education is to let loose in the minds, particularly of the promising young people of the country, whether Christian or otherwise, a flood of Christian ideals which will so influence their thinking that whether they become Christians or not they will go out and seek to live, partially at least, up to what they have learned, and thus improve the level of society. As a result of their influence, society in time will be so leavened that more and more people will be inclined toward the acceptance of the Christian religion and thus be brought into a real Christian faith. It is the earnest hope and desire that many of the students while attending Christian institutions will themselves become Christians.

2. *The Training of Children from Christian Homes to Become Church Leaders.* The second view takes the position that the missions or missionaries do not accept as their responsibility, save in a secondary and indirect way, either the leavening of society with Christian ideals or opening up the way for non-Christian young people to obtain a Christian education, but they are ready to do everything possible to prepare leaders for the church from the Christian constituency. Whichever of these views is adopted will very profoundly influence the whole educational program of the mission. If the first view is accepted, from the beginning, schools—both lower schools and high schools, and even colleges—will be planned and started as soon as possible, looking forward to creating a friendly and co-operative

attitude on the part of the future leaders of the country. If the second view is adopted, it will mean that higher forms of education will be initiated only after a Christian constituency has been formed, which needs such education to maintain its influence. Then the purpose of the schools will be primarily to provide facilities for the training of the children of these Christian homes, the great majority of whom will be graduates of Christian lower schools, so that they may become better equipped and prepared for the responsibilities of Christian leadership, which will of necessity be thrust upon them.

In many cases these two aims of missionary education have not been regarded as mutually exclusive and both the training of Christian leaders as well as the impact on society have been in the minds of those who have been in charge of the institutions. However, in the actual working out either one or the other of these two aims will of necessity decide the guiding policy of the management of the institution; and as the purpose of any particular school becomes more strongly directed in either one of these two directions, the alternate one becomes of only very secondary importance. If the impact on society is held to be the primary purpose, then the highest educational standards and the closest possible integration with the viewpoint of the government officials must be maintained at all costs, even though it means the use of non-Christian members on the faculty. On the other hand, if the training of future Christian leaders from among the Christian constituency is the primary object, when necessary the maintenance of the highest educational standards will be sacrificed, at least temporarily, in order that the highest spiritual standards may be preserved in the teaching staff and the strongest possible Christian atmosphere be developed in the student body.

While it is true that many of the famous universities and colleges in mission fields today have been established and are maintained as mission institutions, with the broader and first-mentioned objective as their main purpose, it is the unqualified conviction of the writer that from the point of view of direct results attained in the interests of the cause of Christ and the planting and development of an indigenous church, the narrower objective is the one which should characterize all mission schools. It will of course mean less spectacular and less impressive institutions with much smaller student bodies, but I am convinced that in the long run the results will more than compensate.

Educational Work and the Indigenous Church

The great need for an adequate educational policy in order to establish an indigenous church has sometimes been lost sight of in missionary planning for the planting of a church and some of the larger non-denominational missions are only recently realizing the grave consequences of failure to make sufficient provision for the training of the future church leaders.

As has already been pointed out, one of the secrets for the successful planting of an indigenous church is the producing of well-trained, consecrated leaders. In order to do this, it will require that the mission, or missions, in each territory see to it that Christian schools of good educational standards are established. Where this is not done the children from Christian homes will be forced to attend government or other non-Christian institutions, which in the mission field always means anti-Christian schools, where their faith will be under constant attack and all incentive to go into active Christian work is in grave danger of being undermined and swept away.

The degree of the education which is provided in the mission schools will naturally depend upon the conditions and degree of civilization of the people concerned. It should be clear however that in each field the mission or missions at work should see to it that at least one school is established and maintained that shall be of equal educational standards with any government or non-Christian school. In recent years with the great advance made in even backward countries along educational lines, it will probably mean at least one Christian school of high school grade, with plans to increase it in a few years to collegiate status. Only as pastors and Christian laymen are well educated in Christian schools can they expect to gain and maintain the respect of the people to whom they minister and still more to gain the hearing of the non-Christian population.

The high school and college age is the critical time in the Christian life of young people everywhere. It is useless for a mission or church to make ample provision for education of the children of Christians up to the sixth or eighth grades and then to stop. For, if there are government high schools and colleges which the brighter and more ambitious students can enter, it will mean that those who continue their education will be largely lost to the Church, at least as active workers. Another result of this short-sighted policy will be that graduates from the higher institutions will look down upon the church leaders and will feel that the gospel and the church have an appeal only for people of lower educational status.

While educational institutions of higher grades are always matters of heavy expense, especially in their first establishment, it is an expense that is well justified in view of the future returns, and particularly so if the schools are maintained on a high spiritual plane as well as high academic standards.

Care should be taken when the mission erects school buildings that they are not too far advanced either in style or architecture or equipment. Nothing should be done that will greatly postpone the time when the nationals will themselves be ready to take over the schools and their management and support.

Essentials for a Truly "Christian School"

As to what constitutes a Christian school, there is a wide divergence of opinion. It must be admitted at the beginning that it is one thing to lay down rules as to what is necessary for a truly Christian school, and it is quite another thing to carry them out in practice. Certainly, however, the standards must include the following.

A Faculty That Is Entirely Christian. In the Orient there is a relationship between teacher and pupil which is quite unknown in this country. In some lands the highest possible title that can be given by a younger to an older man is that of "Teacher" and a very close bond nearly always exists between the two. Therefore, when non-Christian faculty members are found in a mission or in a so-called Christian institution, their influence on the students must have a strongly deterring effect when it comes to accepting Jesus Christ as Saviour and Lord and an open adoption of the Christian faith.

Every non-Christian member of the faculty in a mission or Christian institution therefore which has as its purpose the objective of training Christian leadership, is a glaring inconsistency and exerts an influence which is essentially in direct opposition to the purpose for which the school was founded. This is a fact which cannot be over-emphasized.

A Predominantly Christian Student Body. The atmosphere of a school is created not only by the principal and faculty but fully as much by the students themselves. Then in order to have anything like a true Christian atmosphere in the school, it can only be brought about when sixty-five to seventy-five per cent of the students are professing Christians or at least come from Christian homes. Only then can the religious exercises be carried on in an atmosphere of reverence and worship. I have more than once been present at chapel exercises in mission high schools where the students were largely non-Christian. In spite of the earnest talks given by members of the faculty, it was painful to notice the inattention of the students. This often was aggravated by conversation, irreverence, and various forms of unruly conduct, which destroyed any atmosphere of worship and made it almost impossible even for the earnest Christians present to receive any real blessing.

A Positive Christian Atmosphere. To maintain a positive Christian atmosphere in a school means a never-ending drive on the part of the principal himself together with a co-operative faculty. As a general thing, it is the responsibility of the principal to set the pace in maintaining the standards, and only as he is known by his faculty and students as a man who is wholly consecrated himself, will the atmosphere be actively and positively Christian. It will mean that Bible study is a regular part of the curriculum and that attendance at chapel exercises will be required of all the students. The whole purpose will be to make Christ real as the living Lord to every student. When this is done, the results in the lives of the students are amazing and they in turn become imbued with the desire to go out and preach Christ to their own people. The converse is equally true: when the majority of the students are non-Christians, or when the principal and faculty do not have a strong and effective Christian witness, the atmosphere of the school becomes not a help but a positive hindrance to the development of Christian life and character of even the students from Christian homes.

Problems in Mission Educational Work

Problems in mission educational work have become increasingly acute in practically every mission field, and they touch almost every phase of the work. The two most difficult questions are but briefly treated here.

Governmental Attitude and Regulations. For a number of years in many lands, the carrying on of mission schools has become increasingly difficult. Missionary leaders have realized only too clearly that the day for missionary educational institutions is fast closing. In recent years when national self-consciousness has been rising so strongly everywhere and where national suspicion has been fomented by propaganda of various kinds, the governments of these countries have become increasingly convinced that they themselves must take over the responsibility of educating their own children and young people and that they cannot afford to risk putting their education into the hands of foreigners, particularly of foreign missionaries who are in that country openly for the purpose of converting people to the Christian faith. So often Christian convictions and the Spirit of Christ run completely contrary to the ideals and national customs of the heathen countries and their governments.

Japan was one of the first countries to take that attitude and for over twenty-five or thirty years now foreign missions have not been allowed to conduct any lower schools, although the door has not been closed for high schools and colleges. Within the last decade Persia has taken a similar attitude and has practically taken over all the mission educational institutions, buying out the property from the missions concerned and making them purely national institutions. With this changing attitude on the part of governments, many new regulations have been put into effect which have made it increasingly difficult for the missions to carry on schools that were in a real sense Christian. Such regulations, for instance notably in Japan, required the employment of teachers who could meet certain governmental educational requirements. As this meant they must be graduates of government institutions, it was almost impossible on certain occasions to secure Christian men and women of whom the government would approve. In the same way the government decided on the required curriculum, which meant that there was no time or place left for Bible study, officially recognized as such. The increasing pressure in those schools, which were recognized by the government as educationally on a par with their own, forbade them in a number of cases to have any religious exercises in the buildings or on the school premises. As time went by, increasing pressure was put on the institutions, insisting that faculty and students should go out to the state Shinto shrines to do obeisance to the sun goddess. Things became more acute until it was recognized by missionary leaders in Japan and Korea that it was impossible to carry on really Christian schools. One of the bishops of the Anglican Church in Japan said to me in a private conversation, "A really Christian school is out of the range of possibility now; all we can do is to carry on a school under as nearly Christian auspices as possible." In India while the British were still in authority, government subsidies were granted to certain mission colleges and universities but only on condition that no religious exercises would be required of the students; and now with the withdrawal of the British government, the new India government is claiming that inasmuch as only two per cent of the tax comes from Christians, the government subsidies which were formerly granted to these mission colleges and universities must be very greatly decreased.

Expense. Educational work even under the best of circumstances is always one of the most expensive forms of mission work, and that expense goes up by leaps and bounds as the standards of the schools are raised. In many countries where the church has attained a fair degree of independence and is well established, the church itself is strong enough to maintain the elementary schools for its own children. Whether this is done by the church itself or by substantial Christian nationals is more or less unimportant. When it comes to middle schools or high schools a much greater expense is involved, inasmuch as when government standards are met it is quite impossible to maintain the expenses of an institution solely on the tuition received from the students, and ways and means have to be found whereby large subsidies can be secured, either from mission funds or from wealthy nationals or some other source. When it comes to higher education, the expense is almost prohibitive. Therefore most all colleges and universities are union institutions in which a number of the larger boards and missions carry on the work together.

Results in Educational Work

The results in educational work will in a large measure depend upon the Christian character and aggressiveness of the principal and faculty. This is a truth which it is almost impossible to over-emphasize. More than once we have seen the entire atmosphere of a school changed by a change in the principal, whether missionary or national. It is highly important that any mission undertaking this kind of work should be careful to see that those in charge are men and women not only of faith themselves but of that dynamic variety of faith which will not rest until it sees that Christ is coming into the lives of the students. Only as this is the real goal of the school will it send out young men and women who will be the real Christian leaders of their people, with lives consecrated to serve Him and to win others to Him. From one boys' high school in Syen Chun, in North Korea, the graduates formed the dominating influence in the three presbyteries of that district, both through the many who had become ministers and the still larger number of well-established Christian laymen, whose personal influence and whose gifts were important factors in the life and development of the church throughout the province.

Educational Work Is the Most Expensive Evangelizing Agency. If schools are established primarily for the purpose of evangelizing the heathen and of leavening with Christian ideals the pupils who come there, it should be realized at once that this is one of the most expensive and least productive ways for obtaining those ends. The expense of buildings, both in their construction and maintenance, the salaries of the teachers and all the responsibilities connected with the maintenance of the school are a heavy drain upon the resources of any mission, both in finances and personnel. In schools also where the majority of the students are non-Christians it is often very disappointing to see how few of them really make any profession of faith and accept Christ before they graduate. Not only this, but, as has been stated on numerous occasions in various mission fields, one of the greatest disappointments in connection with those who have received baptism on profession of faith during their school course is the way in which many of them completely disappear shortly after their graduation, many not being heard of again and making no contribution whatsoever to the churches in their home areas or even attending the services. On the other hand, when the schools are maintained for the purpose of educating the children of Christians, just the opposite is the case. In the city of Pyengyang in North Korea, where there was a union Christian college and a high school conducted by the Northern Presbyterian Mission, in both of which institutions the great majority of the students were Christians, about four hundred of the boys went out every Sunday to conduct Sunday schools, preach in missions, lead in country churches and carry on active evangelistic work. Over the years the results of the evangelizing efforts of these students is incalculable.

Some Influential Enemies of the Church Are Graduates of Mission Schools. Among the many non-Christians who attend high schools and colleges founded by missions, with the avowed purpose of converting the students to the Christian faith, the great majority of them enter for the sake of the educational advantages they will receive, with no intention of becoming interested in the gospel. As they harden their hearts to the influences brought upon them during those years, by the time they graduate they are in the position of those who feel that they have been exposed to the influence of Christianity and by their continued indifference to it have convinced themselves that it has little to offer them personally. By reason of their contact with the Christian faculty and students they feel that they are in a position to work against the influence of the gospel even more effectively than if they had never entered the institution. While this reaction is not the normal experience of non-Christian graduates from mission schools, nevertheless some of the most effective and influential enemies of the church are found among them.

Wrong Impressions Are Sometimes Made on Non-Christians Regarding the Real Purpose of Missions and of Foreign Missionaries. In most mission fields as a result of the union work of a number of missions, large and imposing universities and colleges have been established, magnificent buildings have been erected, beautiful campuses laid out, and sometimes the houses of the faculty members have been built to match the school buildings. Very often such houses are on a considerably more elaborate scale than the residences of the missionaries who are engaged in strictly evangelistic and other church work. To the non-Christian it seems very evident that while the missionaries are there, according to their own words, mainly for the purpose of preaching the gospel, the very fact that such tremendous sums are spent in the erection and establishment of these large universities and that the residences connected with them are larger and finer than those of the workers who are engaged in direct evangelistic and church activity, indicates very strongly that in reality the missionaries themselves place more importance on the educational work than in the preaching of the gospel. Also, the dormitories which are built and furnished for the students may get them accustomed to living on a more comfortable scale than they have any expectation of being able to maintain after graduation. Graduates of girls' colleges and girls' high schools in several mission fields have more than once been reported as being quite unwilling to consider marriage to pastors or to theological students because of the impossibility of being able to continue to live in the manner in which they have been accustomed while they have been in school. As a result, many of these girls marry into non-Christian families and to all useful purposes are lost to the church.

In this presentation of the arguments which have been advanced against the plan of education for education's sake and especially among non-Christian students, it is only fair to say that a tremendous and often incalculable indirect influence has been exerted by these colleges and universities. Especially in Moslem lands have they done much to bring about a more sympathetic understanding on the part of the Mohammedan population and have helped greatly to break down the barriers of opposition and antipathy towards the Christian religion and towards the gospel.

RELATION OF THE SCHOOLS TO THE INDIGENOUS CHURCH

In much of Korea all lower schools, from the beginning, were in the hands of the church and were not started or controlled by missionaries or the missions at any time. This would seem to be the ideal way of educational work of that grade anywhere, if it is at all possible. In most countries now the people themselves have come to realize the importance of education for their children and in the majority of cases, when the Christian constituency is of some size they are able to pay the expenses necessary to maintain schools of primary grade. When it comes to higher education or specialized education such as theological seminaries and Bible institutes, the missions must usually take the initial step to establish such schools, with the view however to their eventually being taken over by the national church. There will be two steps in this process. The first step is that of forming joint boards of directors; both foreign missionaries and nationals of real faith and standing should be elected to these boards. In this way the nationals will be brought to a place of understanding the educational needs, the work of the institutions, the qualifications for faculty and students, and the other problems connected with administration and carrying on of such schools. Many times these members will be found to be of great value in giving suggestions as to how to meet certain specific problems, especially those which arise in connection with the personnel, and also in regard to winning the confidence of the church. The second step is a much slower one in which the national churches will begin to support and finally take over full maintenance of the institutions. This is a problem which has to be worked out with great care and patience and with the advice and help of the national members of the board. It may start out with special offerings made by the churches. In some cases the churches themselves will elect or appoint their representatives on the board of directors, in which case those men will go directly to the church bodies which they represent and present the needs to them and the necessity for their assuming a part, however small, at the beginning, toward meeting the financial responsibilities of the institution. As the institution grows and the national Christians understand its value, often those of wealth can be found who will give generously of their means and their property toward endowment for the school. Just as soon as the nationals are able to maintain the financial support as well as the educational and spiritual standards, the missions should be only too glad to turn over the buildings and other properties to them and allow them to assume full responsibility for the maintenance and direction of the schools.

QUESTIONS FOR DISCUSSION

1. What are the two views of the aim of missionary educational work? Can they be carried on simultaneously? Discuss their respective merits and weaknesses.
2. What are the essentials to make a school truly Christian? How can they be attained and how can the Christian atmosphere be maintained?
3. Discuss the main problems in mission schools which arise from the attitudes and regulations of the governments.
4. Discuss the relationship of schools to the indigenous church program and outline steps that should be taken to place the schools on an indigenous basis as soon as possible.

CHAPTER XIV

RELATIONS BETWEEN FOREIGN MISSIONARIES AND THE NATIONAL CHURCHES

GOAL OF THE FOREIGN MISSIONARY: TO MAKE HIMSELF UNNECESSARY

THE GOAL in missionary work will be achieved only as a church is established which is independent and indigenous. This objective should be kept continually in the thought and prayers of every missionary, and the missionary and the mission should plan to reach it as soon as possible. I have been impressed in reading some missionary literature by the way foreign missionaries of decades of experience have been thinking and planning about their successors. Every foreign missionary should so plan and so carry on his work under the leadership of the Holy Spirit that there should be no need for a missionary successor to him when he comes to lay down his work. I mean by that that he should be so interested and active in planning for his work to be taken over by national Christians and so careful in his training them for that work that in many cases while it may be necessary for other foreign missionaries to come and live at the station, there will be no need for them to take over the particular work which he has been doing. That work should be in the hands of those whom he has brought up in the faith.

NECESSITY FOR THE MISSIONARY TO DECREASE AS RESULTS INCREASE

Even though repeating what has already been said, let me say again that indispensability is not the sign of a successful work. No foreign missionary therefore should make himself indispensable. On the contrary, he should plan to make his presence unnecessary as soon as possible. With this in view, he should always be alert and ready to withdraw himself from various kinds of work and offices just as soon as conditions warrant such a step. He thereby becomes free to undertake new forms of work in that area or to begin pioneer work in some other district. He should therefore be eager to withdraw from all the following phases.

Work Which the Nationals Are Ready to Assume. When we say "ready" we mean work which they themselves are willing to take over and are able to administer. This does not mean that at first they will carry on the work as efficiently as the foreign missionary; but nevertheless if they can take it over with a reasonable prospect of success, it should be turned over to them and left in their hands, with the missionary being ready to stand behind them and to work with them when necessary until they have gained the experience and confidence to carry on entirely alone.

Positions of Church Authority Unless Chosen By the Nationals Themselves. As the national church develops in wisdom and power, it should assume responsibility for the conduct of its own work. In that case foreign missionaries should act as pastors of churches only when they have been so elected or appointed by the conference or the presbytery in charge of the district. In several mission fields in recent years the foreign missionaries have been requested by the national churches to assume the responsibility for the less evangelized districts and to take the oversight of the unorganized groups and also those which though organized were not sufficiently strong to undertake the support of a fully-ordained pastor. When a church developed to the degree that it was able to support a pastor of its own, the missionary in charge gladly resigned his position as pastor and withdrew his connection, unless there was a special request for him to remain on as co-pastor. Co-pastoral relations have proved very successful and very helpful; in these cases the foreign missionary acts on an equality with his brother minister, giving advice whenever necessary and preaching when invited, but being careful to advance his brother and to take for himself a place of secondary importance.

Established Work in Order to Undertake New Activities. As the regular church work and the various churches which have been established are taken over by the national pastors, the missionaries are thereby freed to do pioneer work, opening up new territories, and beginning new types of work in fields already opened. This new work may be unevangelized districts in not too far distant areas or it may include undertaking work among new classes of people who have as yet been unreached by the gospel.

Often men have done very successful work in opening up special classes among the government officials or among the priests of the national religions or, where the caste system prevails, among certain groups of untouchables or low class of people who have not as yet felt free to mingle with the others.

As Western civilization comes in, new and large groups of people are formed, who by the nature of their work are very often rendered almost unreachable by the gospel in the usual ways. I refer to those in the large factories and mills; in many cases they enter these places for three to five years and hardly come out during that time. In many of the Far Eastern ports, with the growth of buses and street cars, girl conductors are a recent innovation; also there are those working in cafes, another mark of Western civilization, and other similar groups, most of whom, at least for some time to come, will require special efforts and special types of evangelization.

As a general thing it will be the foreign missionaries, whose eyes are open to all such new possibilities, that will have to take the leading part and do the pioneer work in these areas. As the various degrees of withdrawal mentioned above are put into effect, it will of course be necessary for the foreign missionary to be sympathetic at all times and ready to give advice or help wherever needed. Human nature all over the world is the same and almost always when the national Christians or leaders find the missionary is willing to withdraw, they honor him that much more; very cordial relations follow and usually appeals to him for advice and help after he has withdrawn are more numerous than before. The reverse also can be true. Where the missionary is unwilling to withdraw voluntarily and has to be almost forced out, it often takes years before the adjustment is made and before the nationals are able to realize with gratitude the value of the service he has rendered and the blessing that could be received from him in helpful advice.

Again it must be emphasized that this willingness to push his national brother forward while he himself takes a lesser place requires the continual exercise of real grace by the average foreign missionary, grace mingled with true humility. I believe that our mission boards and committees, as they are examining candidates for missionary service, should stress in the future much more than they have in the past the matter of humility as one of the most important qualifications for successful missionary work. It is a grace, alas, for which Anglo-Saxons are not noted, and unquestionably the lack of it has been a frequent reason for misunderstanding and for lack of successful growth in many mission churches established during the past century. In the Orient today humility is still regarded as one of the signs of a great man. I remember that more than once I have heard Oriental Christians discussing others, whether missionaries or members of their own race, and saying that in their opinion, a certain individual was a great man, unquestionably so. On being asked the reason, the reply was that he was so humble, and that only a great man can be truly humble.

On one occasion, at the request of an unordained church worker in a certain village, I called upon one of the leading men, a gentleman of great influence who had been bitter in his persecution of the church, which he regarded as a Western religion, in opposition to the Confucianism of his family and his ancestors for generations. I agreed to go to see him and sat for an hour and a half or more in the guest room. Almost the whole time he was carrying on a spirited conversation with one of his friends who had arrived there before I did. The discussions covered a wide range of subjects, including Confucianism and Confucian beliefs and the differences in Christianity, Western habits, and customs; but the conversation was kept up at such a tempo that it was almost impossible for me to get in any word at all. At the end of an hour and a half I bade my host farewell and came away feeling that I had utterly failed as an ambassador of the Lord Jesus Christ and that nothing had been gained whatsoever by my visit. To my surprise, word came to me the following day that I had made a tremendous impression and that the enmity and the opposition towards the church was apparently removed. And this proved true. I learned that immediately after I had left, my host began praising me to his friend and his family. The very fact that I had been humble enough to sit there and listen to him talk for all that time without losing my temper or showing signs of being offended gave him the idea that there was something great about me. He said of me, "He is the first Westerner I have seen that was humble!" Perhaps the only Westerners he had seen previously were a few exploiters, and it was understandable how their attitude would be different from mine.

The whole question of withdrawing and transferring responsibilities to the national Christian leaders requires not only grace and humility but flexibility on the part of each individual foreign missionary and the missionary body as a whole. As the growing church takes over responsibilities and authorities, it means that the attitude of the missionary in vital relation to it must continually be changing, as he gives over the work which he has been used by God to establish and to develop. It is at this point that one of the commonest causes for criticism on the part of the national leaders concerning missionaries is found. On a number of occasions toward the end of my service in Korea some of the pastors and other leaders came to me and frankly discussed the missionaries and our work and our relationship to them. Perhaps the most often-heard criticism was this, "We can never forget or over-state our appreciation and gratitude to the older missionaries who came out and brought to our people the gospel and all that it has meant in salvation, in new life, and light. They are our spiritual fathers and mothers in Christ and for that we shall always be thankful, but we do feel that often they have failed to realize and still fail to realize that we are growing up spiritually and are now in a position to take over the responsibility and make our own decisions and plans for our church, rather than leaving it all in their hands." I think it will be fair to say that one of the besetting sins of most missionaries is lack of flexibility and readiness to recognize the growth and development of the people whom they have won to the Lord and trained in service.

In order to keep relations cordial and harmonious and at the same time encourage the growth of an independent and indigenous church, each missionary needs to feel called of God to continue to examine himself and his heart in regard to this matter and to see to it that there is no desire within him to hold on to the reins of authority any longer than is absolutely necessary. The Lord will then raise up the leaders to carry on the work of their own church.

QUESTIONS FOR DISCUSSION

1. State and discuss what should be the goal of every foreign missionary. Outline what it will require on the part of the missionary and how it will affect his attitude and relationship to his brethren among the national Christians.

2. Discuss the various positions and types of work from which

the foreign missionary should definitely plan to withdraw, and how this can most satisfactorily be done.

3. State types of new activity and work which missionaries will naturally be led to undertake with the incoming of Western civilization upon the people.

4. In the light of the subjects discussed in this chapter, what should be increasingly considered as one of the most important qualifications required in every prospective missionary?

Chapter XV

PROBLEMS MET IN THE
INDIGENOUS CHURCH POLICY

THE PROBLEMS we will discuss in this chapter, though met in all types of foreign mission work, are seen more prominently in connection with the carrying on of an indigenous church policy. In carrying on the work as outlined in the previous chapters, the missionary from the beginning discusses with the people the various difficulties which must be overcome; this makes the problems more easily seen. It also means that the attitude and relationship from the beginning between the missionary and the national Christians will be one of frankness and open expression on the part of the people. This is wholesome. All missionary work is a continual struggle, in which the foreign missionary always is, or should be, giving out of himself, his influence, his strength, his spiritual power, and all that he has; and the carrying on of an indigenous church policy means a particularly stern struggle, especially at the beginning, and demands a continued watchfulness on the part of the missionary until the church is firmly planted and its own independent life develops.

THE POVERTY OF THE PEOPLE

The grinding poverty of the great mass of the people in practically every mission field exerts a continual pressure upon the sympathies of the missionary. In many lands today the equivalent of thirty cents is a good average day's wage. In large parts of Korea a few years ago, one hundred and fifty dollars would represent the total income of the average family of five persons, that is, thirty dollars per year on which to feed and house and clothe each member. In many families it would average even less than that. In the face of this constant poverty, it seems at first almost heartless to insist upon the people supporting their workers and putting up their own churches and buildings; and yet this must be done if the work is to develop. Poverty never holds back people from engaging in idolatrous worship and from making their contributions for carrying on temple ceremonies and other superstitious practices; in fact, as a result of rather careful investigation, I am convinced that many a heathen in his superstition and idolatry, gives as much or more to the worship of idols as a Christian to the worship and service of the Lord. In a good many places offerings are taken, not in money but in grain, especially among the women who seldom have any money coming into their possession, and particularly in those countries where barter is the usual method of business. By eating a little less and setting aside one or two spoonfuls from each meal for the service of the Lord and the work of the church, it is surprising how much comes in. Again and again wedding rings, the only article of jewelry that many of the women in the Orient possess, are found in the offering boxes. When the love of the Lord really gets into the hearts of men and women, as they realize His great sacrifice and how much it has meant to them, nothing is too valuable to give to Him; and there is a joy in presenting the offering, a joy often lacking among people in this land of comforts and luxuries.

Following the Line of Least Resistance

In view of the great poverty, both material and spiritual, which always goes with heathenism, and loneliness which at one time or another bears down heavily upon every foreign missionary, there is a continual struggle against the urge to yield to some of the many and often pathetic pleas of the nationals for assistance. In the Orient, as I suppose in almost all pagan countries, individualism as we know it in the West is very rare. The family or the clan is the seat of authority, and they have therefore been brought up to lean upon each other, and to seek advice and comfort and help of all kinds from their relatives. When the foreign missionary therefore identifies himself in his faith and interests and service with a group of new believers, it is only natural for them to turn to him and to come to him for assistance of almost every variety and to press hard upon his sympathies in ways to which he is entirely unaccustomed and to which therefore it is all the more difficult for him to turn a deaf ear. Not only this, but in addition to the spirit of dependence there is one of bargaining. This means that when a man comes to ask assistance he will nearly always ask for double or more than what he expects to get. Very often in doing so he is entirely unconscious of any moral defect or inconsistency in carrying out a lifetime custom. This necessitates what must often seem to the new missionary an attitude of heartless indifference in turning a deaf ear to apparently earnest pleas; yet it is one that is absolutely necessary at times, in the interests of teaching the young Christians and churches to stand on their own feet and to develop a spirit of independence and initiative.

The Paternalistic Attitude of Foreign Missionaries. The late Dr. Cleland B. McAfee used to warn missionaries against the danger of having the "downward slant" in their attitude toward the people among whom they were working. When constantly appealed to for various kinds of help and advice, it is very easy unconsciously to take on an attitude of pride and especially of spiritual pride toward the people. Personally, I have noticed again and again that those missionaries who constantly speak of the people as "our Christians," "our Japanese," or "our Koreans," are very often those who most easily adopt this attitude. Unconsciously, as a missionary begins to think for and to plan for the people in whose welfare he has become so vitally interested, he is in danger of coming to regard them as incapable of thoroughly planning for themselves, and as being in large measure therefore dependent upon him. This in itself works against the development of the indigenous church. It is a subtle temptation and demands constant watchfulness. Roland Allen speaks of the love of administration as "the besetting sin of European missionaries." As a missionary's influence grows and he is regarded by the people as the head of a given work, he easily comes to regard himself in the same light, and almost unconsciously he acquires the airs and authority of an administrator, rather than the consciousness that he is there only temporarily and that he is soon to transfer the authority and administrative responsibility to his brethren.

RACIAL CONSCIOUSNESS

With the rapid upsurge of national and racial consciousness in recent years in all lands, the prestige of the white race has been correspondingly lowered. The tremendous victory of the Japanese army and navy in the beginning of the second World War and the fact that in the previous World War the white race and the so-called Christian nations were fighting among themselves significantly lowered the general standing of the white peoples. As a result, there has been a super-sensitiveness on the part of the national Christians and an unwarranted readiness to feel insulted or injured. In Korea some of the missionaries were able to consult with one of the outstanding national Christians, a member of the old Korean aristocracy but who had studied in America and received a doctor of philosophy degree in this country. They asked him to tell them frankly how missionaries were most prone to hurt the feelings of their Korean brethren. The information he graciously gave them was passed on to new missionaries to enable them to avoid making the same mistakes as had their predecessors. Such matters as wearing second-best clothes when invited out to preach or to meals in the homes of Koreans; speaking to each other in English in the presence of Koreans, who of course were unable then to follow the conversation; the slightness of their bows toward elderly Koreans, who were accustomed to receiving a low bow from their younger friends—these were especially emphasized.

Japanese officials often sharply criticized Westerners in regard to their manner of making salutations, and their failure to greet them with the low, reverential bows which they expected. Brusqueness in speech and the habit of going straight to the point is something which is still foreign to many Oriental minds—after centuries of formal salutations and a gradual approach to the main subject of conversation. Care concerning these matters and many others of local application is often what makes the difference between a missionary whose success is mediocre and the one who quickly wins the confidence in those countries of believers and non-Christians alike, and is recognized as a person of understanding and sympathy.

From now on greater effort should be made by new missionaries not only to learn the language well but to become familiar with the customs and etiquette of the people. In previous years the national Christians were ready to overlook the ignorance on the part of missionaries in regard to these things, but with the rising of national self-consciousness they are much more critical and demand very much more from their missionary friends than heretofore. This is a matter which cannot be overlooked and missions need to emphasize its importance increasingly in their training of new workers.

EVANGELIZATION NOT WESTERNIZATION

We must always remember that the aim of missionaries

is to evangelize, not to Westernize. There is sometimes a tendency to forget the wide difference between the two and to think that to introduce Christianity means also to introduce Western ways of life. In some of the oriental countries, especially, this has become a real problem and missionaries should be careful not to press the introducing of Western methods and gadgets along with presenting the gospel and winning the people to the Lord Jesus Christ. As the gospel enters the lives of the people, it will naturally change many of their customs, but it must be understood that it is the gospel that is making the change and not the Western missionaries.

The Danger of Favoritism

Another matter which should be guarded against is that of relying too much upon the advice and counsel of one or two individuals among the national Christians. It is very easy to make "pets" of some who are particularly congenial, by giving too much attention to them and relying too much on their advice. As this occurs, not only may they develop an attitude of spiritual pride, but through their intimacy with the missionary they may become alienated from their own people, and rifts may easily arise between the missionary and the people whom he is seeking to win. Almost any missionary of much experience can recall unhappy relationships which have occurred from this cause.

The "Real Estate" Problem

A well-built house is necessary to preserve the health and morale of the missionary and sufficient property around it to allow for gardens and for breathing space is also advisable. Yet these things can be overdone and imposing mission compounds and residences may overshadow the spirit and the real purpose of the missionaries and become a barrier between them and the people. As a general rule, however, it is not nearly so much the buildings and the property which are the barriers as is the way in which they are used. The spirit reflected by the missionary who lives in them is the thing which is going to count most. The more pretentious the buildings, of course, the more ready the missionary must be to manifest that spirit of humility and of friendship which will make the national Christians feel at home and welcome in spite of surroundings which would otherwise tend to over-awe. As has been pointed out by

Roland Allen and others, the possession by missions of large properties always tends to increase administrative responsibilities and time is required to see that the properties are kept up, and in some countries special care has to be taken to see that the nationals do not exercise squatters' rights. In the rental of mission property to nationals, whether Christian or non-Christian, particular care must be exercised. It is surprisingly easy for friction and bitterness to arise between the missionary and his tenants, especially where economic conditions are difficult. Whenever some national feels that a foreign missionary is "making money" out of such an arrangement, trouble is sure to follow, and lasting scars in the memories on both sides are almost inevitable.

QUESTIONS FOR DISCUSSION

1. Discuss some particular problems arising out of the poverty of the people, showing the mistakes which missionaries might make in meeting them.
2. Discuss why a paternalistic attitude on the part of the missionaries is likely to arise, and how it can be avoided.
3. Distinguish between Evangelization and Westernization, giving illustrations of each.
4. Discuss the "Real Estate Problem" and make suggestions as to how it may be solved.

CHAPTER XVI

THE RESULTS OF AN INDIGENOUS
CHURCH POLICY

SOME OF THE many valuable results that come from
pursuing consistently an indigenous church policy are considered in this chapter.

A Stronger and More Aggressive Church

This means, in the first place, that a church is established
which from the beginning will learn to stand on its own feet,
make its own decisions, pursue its own policies, and carry on an
aggressive, evangelistic, forward-looking program of its own,
one adapted to the conditions and the thoughts of the people
among whom it is working. It is a church characterized from
the start by national workers, for leaders only develop as responsibility is placed upon them and as they learn to exercise
initiative under the guidance of the Holy Spirit. As long as
the foreign missionary retains the leadership it is difficult for
national leadership to develop. Until the missionary shows a
readiness to turn over the responsibilities of the work to the
church members, leaders from among them will be the exception rather than the rule. They will be few; because unless
a policy similar to what we have been discussing in the previous
chapters is carried out, the new Christians will naturally look
to the foreign missionary for advice and for the support of the
work. They will naturally turn to him as the one to make the
decisions, and thereby they will become trained from the beginning not to solve their own problems, nor to think for themselves, but to depend upon outsiders for leadership. This gen-
erates two difficulties; for just as the missionary is training the
national Christian to look to him for leadership, he is also
unconsciously training himself to expect to continue to lead and
the longer he holds that attitude, the more difficult it is for him
to appreciate the potential ability of the church members, and
to turn over to them the authority he has been wielding. For
that reason, as has been mentioned previously, it may well mean
that heroic steps must be taken with this old-line policy in order

to initiate the newer policy for the establishment of an indigenous church.

As the method which we have been advocating is employed, not only will it make for a stronger and more aggressive church, but it will make for the development of leadership and initiative among the individuals themselves. As we have seen, when from the beginning of each new group its members fully understand that the group is theirs and the responsibility for leadership and of making the decisions rests with them, the development of leadership begins immediately. There is no period therefore in its history in which its members will depend entirely upon missionary directions. I well remember visiting two mission fields, divided only by a river, in which the two policies of work had been consistently carried on. In one field, after over thirty years of work, the first pastor was being ordained. In the other field, after less than twenty years of work, there were over one hundred ordained pastors carrying on their work in entire independence of foreign supervision. I am confident that the main reason for the vast difference in the development in these two fields was the difference in policy and outlook and attitude of the missionaries.

A More Rapid Growth

The carrying on of an indigenous church policy will mean a much more rapid growth when once the foundations have been laid. The process of laying the foundation will possibly take longer, for it is always so much easier to win converts and to gain a following when money is forthcoming to supply the salaries of those who will exercise pastoral care and to provide church buildings. As has already been noted, these things in themselves often create a wrong emphasis in the minds of the early converts, and the new believers may take their stand as much from the motive of possible physical or social benefits as from true faith and a real spiritual understanding of their need for the Lord Jesus. When the two methods have been carried on side by side in neighboring territories, in the one where the old-line policy was used during the first decade or so, the number of converts was much larger than where the indigenous church policy was used. However, after the first decade was past and the foundation laid, in the territory where the indigenous church policy was practiced, progress was made by leaps and bounds. For as each convert was won he or she became in

turn an aggressive worker to go out and win others on his own
initiative rather than waiting until he had been directed to do
so by a foreign missionary who, perhaps with a little urging,
had been persuaded to grant some financial help in order to
insure this greater activity.

More Wholesome Relations Between Missionaries and Nationals

Not only is there much more rapid growth in the development of the church, but there are far happier and more sincere
relations between the missionaries and the nationals. This is
brought about through the fact that from the beginning they
have worked together as equals and co-laborers. From the
beginning the nationals are chosen by their own people as representatives to collaborate with the foreign missionary in the
government, development, and extension of the church. From
the beginning they regard the church as their work and their
responsibility; therefore, there is no impatient waiting on their
part to have such responsibility turned over to them. When
foreign missionaries are slow to hand over authority, for whatever the reasons, it brings about an unhappy feeling on the
part of the nationals, which may easily cause a real cleavage
in the work. When that kind of inferiority complex has once
been developed in the minds of the nationals, they often mis-
interpret and misunderstand the actions and words of their
missionaries—as many of us have learned through painful experience. In consequence, when the matter finally comes to a
head and the question is discussed openly, the misunderstandings and injured feelings that have previously been held in
abeyance are often over-expressed, causing harm and further
misunderstandings. Such experiences can be avoided.

A More Effective Presentation of the Gospel

Another result of this new policy is what might be described
as a more effective presentation of the gospel. Each people has
its own national characteristics in the interpretation of the gospel
and its application to personal daily living. It is only as the
gospel is presented in the language of the people and in a manner adapted to their mode of thinking and living that it takes
hold of them. Therefore, as the gospel is preached by the people
themselves and revealed in their lives, its impact upon the listeners will be far greater and its results far more rapid than

when it is heard through the medium of a foreigner. This was very forcibly brought to my attention on one occasion when I listened to an address given by a prominent Salvation Army official from England to a group of country folk in Korea. The address fortunately was given in English and interpreted by an unusually gifted Korean. As I sat and listened, if I closed my eyes, I could easily imagine that I was back in London, sitting in a city mission, listening to an address given to a group of drunkards and down-and-outs. It was characterized by a phraseology and viewpoint thoroughly suited to them but poles apart from that of the country people in the Orient where it was being presented. The interpreter, however, understanding the situation, and having an unusual understanding of the English language, was able as he interpreted to change the whole viewpoint and the vocabulary sufficiently to make it at least partially intelligible to the audience. Often as I have listened to missionaries speaking and then to national pastors speaking, that same thing has been impressed on me. Each nationality and each race has its own characteristic temperament to which certain phases of the gospel will make special appeal and to which it will have a particular application.

In the city of Pyengyang, which was the great center of Christianity in Northern Korea until the Russian Army occupied that part of the country, twenty-three Presbyterian churches had grown up in that city itself, during the forty-five years of the missionary activity of that great pioneer, the late Dr. Samuel A. Moffett; and each church supported its own pastor. Over three hundred churches had also been planted in the surrounding area, all of them self-supporting and indigenous. The twenty-three city pastors together with the ordained foreign missionaries formed a City Pastors' Association, which met each month for prayer and conference. In one of their meetings one of the men said, "Brethren, we are getting cold; we need a revival to get us warmed up; what can we do about it?"

A committee was appointed which brought in recommendations which were unanimously adopted. The committee spoke of the peculiar emphasis of the number "forty" in the Scriptures —Moses spent forty days on Mount Sinai, Israel forty years in the wilderness, the Lord was tempted for forty days, there were forty days between the Resurrection and the Ascension, and other "forty" instances. The committee then recommended that a forty-day schedule for prayer be drawn up and a copy distributed to every Christian home in the city, designating for each day a special subject for prayer. Following the forty days of prayer, it was recommended that five days of special meetings be held on behalf of the church officers and Sunday school teachers; for unless they were spiritually warm it was useless to hope for much on the part of the rank and file of the members. That was in turn to be followed by a week of similar union meetings for the church members, which should precede a week's evangelistic campaign in every one of the twenty-three Presbyterian churches in the city.

The committee asked me to speak at the meetings for the church officers. Attendance at those services was limited to church officers, Bible women, and Sunday school teachers. We met at 7:00 A.M. and 7:00 P.M. for an hour of Bible study and prayer. On the opening morning the committee in charge apologized profusely for the small number present—only 300! On the last two days between 900 and 1,000 were at the morning services and 1,300 in the evening meetings. At the joint service on Sunday evening over 6,000 were present in the college gymnasium, and hundreds were turned away. The crowds increased during the following week, when a Korean pastor addressed the gatherings, and the churches of Pyengyang were "warmed"! It was a program planned entirely by nationals, who knew the best way to impress their own people and to gain the desired results.

The sooner the national leaders are trained to plan their own work, the sooner will that presentation of the gospel be forthcoming which is best adapted to the needs of their people.

A Wide Outreach

Another of the important results of this indigenous church policy will be a far wider outreach for each individual missionary. Instead of confining himself to the care of a comparatively small number of churches or groups of Christians, he will—through the national leaders in whose training he has had an integral part—be in touch with scores and even hundreds of churches. His counsel and influence will be multiplied many times through those whom he has trained and who have gone forth, many on their own initiative, to carry on the work which he started.

OPPORTUNITIES FOR NEW TYPES OF WORK

Another result of a consistent indigenous church policy is that it gives the missionary time for opening up new forms of work instead of being tied down with the routine care of the local churches under his jurisdiction. It is easy for a missionary to become bogged down in his own particular field and so tied up with routine that vision and openings for reaching out into untouched territory recede almost to the vanishing point. In an indigenous church policy, however, this routine work is almost all turned over to the local church workers. Thus the foreign missionary has opportunities for learning the needs of his outlying territory and of initiating new work there.

QUESTIONS FOR DISCUSSION

1. Discuss the results of an Indigenous Church Policy as they will affect the aggressiveness and the rapidity of the growth in a church so established.

2. In what way does this type of policy affect the relations between missionaries and the nationals?

3. Discuss some of the new types of work which you think might profitably be initiated in the fields with which you are familiar.

Chapter XVII

PAUL THE MISSIONARY,
AND THE PROBLEMS HE FACED

Perplexities With No Human Resources

A STUDY OF the problems which the Apostle Paul faced in his work as a missionary throughout the Roman Empire will reveal how very similar they were to those commonly experienced today on the foreign mission field.

Idolatry. In Paul's day idolatry was one of the greatest foes of the gospel. Today also it is exerting an enormous influence throughout the heathen world. The great temples to the deities in Athens, in Macedonia, and elsewhere, were monuments to the awful power of idolatry among people in those days. In his First Epistle to the Corinthians, the tenth chapter and the nineteenth and twentieth verses, Paul makes a statement which gives an indication, at least, as to the secret of the tremendous power of the idols in the lives of their worshipers. He writes, "What say I then? that a thing sacrificed to idols is anything, or that an idol is anything? But I say, that the things which the Gentiles sacrifice, they sacrifice to demons, and not to God; and I would not that ye should have communion with demons." In these words Paul is saying that the sacrifices offered to idols by the heathen are not offered so much to the idols themselves as they are to the evil spirits behind the idols, and surely this is the secret of the power of idolatry. It is not the image of wood or stone but the demon spirit behind it which has exercised through the centuries the powerful control it has over the lives and the imaginations of those who worship it. One feature of idolatry which we need to remember is that where it is practiced, superstitious beliefs permeate practically every phase of life, and present perplexing problems to a young Christian. Some of these are referred to in the epistles of the New Testament. These practices in Paul's day concerned the social customs, where often before feasts, food was first offered to the idols, and the problem thereby was raised as to whether or not a Christian could conscientiously partake of food which had been so presented. Paul refers to this in I Corinthians 10 and in Romans 14. In many lands today, as was doubtless true then also, in farming districts where the villagers do the work together, the day starts and ends with some kind of sacrifice to the spirits of fertility, or good luck, or to the goddess of rain, in order that bountiful harvests may come. A very real problem which Christians have had to face throughout the Orient is that of taxes for the erection and maintenance of the shrines and temples. All these things Paul had to face, and in his letters he lays down the principles by which the Christians can meet these questions and make the decisions which will be to the glory of God and to the upbuilding of their own faith.

Slavery. In Paul's day we are told that in Rome only one in every four persons was a free man; and thus the number of slaves was enormous. Then added to the problem of numbers was the fact that in most cases they were of the same color and often of the same social class as their masters—to whose slightest whims they were completely subject. The Epistle to Philemon was written by Paul to his friend concerning Onesimus, a runaway slave, who had fled to Rome and had there come into contact with Paul and had been led to faith in Christ Jesus. According to the Roman law, Philemon had the right to have his runaway slave beaten to death, but Paul sends him back as his own son, beseeching Philemon to receive him as a brother. The fact that in a number of Paul's epistles he gives special instructions on behalf of bondservants or slaves, indicates that many of them were members of the churches. It is interesting to notice that in no case does Paul say anything against the institution of slavery. This was an exhibition of the restraint and wisdom granted to him by the Holy Spirit. It would have been easy to set forth arguments which would inflame and incite rebellion and bring about a bloody revolution, but Paul knew well that in the gospel itself there was a power, which, as it worked out in the lives of those who accepted it, would bring into being those relationships between master and slaves that would so mitigate conditions that the institution itself would be bearable for the time being; but that eventually the institution of slavery as then practiced would be swept away by the power of God inherent in the gospel. Today, while officially slavery does not exist, nevertheless in some lands customs connected with the payment of debts result in various forms of practical slavery which may last for several generations, and present problems similar to those of Paul's day.

Immorality. Another of the tremendous problems which the early church and its missionaries faced was that of immorality. The most terrible immorality is usually associated with idolatry and with slavery. In many of the heathen temples of the ancient world, prostitution was carried on before the idols as a religious rite, as it is in India today, and the influence of such worship upon the lives of the worshipers can better be imagined than described. The fifth chapter of Paul's First Epistle to the Corinthians indicates the depths to which even Christians sank at times in this horrible sin. Wherever the gospel of Jesus Christ has not been known, the curse of Eve upon women still exists today in terrible force. Women have no rights and are regarded purely as the chattels of their husbands, their one responsibility being to cook meals and bear children. In many lands today, childlessness is a recognized reason for divorce. In the course of centuries, because of the low status of women, very strict customs have grown up in many of these lands, separating the sexes, and in some countries, after girls have reached the age of twelve to thirteen they are not allowed to speak to any man, except those to whom they are immediately related until they are married and have borne children of their own. Doubtless, Paul in the early church had to face these problems which are being faced today in many mission fields, problems which have been met and are being worked out under the guidance of the Holy Spirit, as He has given wisdom to the missionary leaders and to the national pastors to take the necessary steps for the moral and spiritual protection of the people and for their guidance in the new life which they have entered.

Suspicion From Officials. Now as then, government officials always look with suspicion upon new religious movements. Being pagans themselves, they cannot understand the underlying motives, and it is very difficult for them to understand what brings the Christian missionary to their land and makes him willing to live under suspicion and misunderstanding and have a real love in his heart for their people. In the histories of many heathen lands new religious movements have caused riots and bloodshed. The officials naturally desire to keep things as far as possible in the *status quo* and regard suspiciously any movement which will cause a change in the beliefs or attitudes of the people whom they are ruling. Paul and the early apostles faced this difficulty again and again, a difficulty which is always augmented, as it was in Paul's day, where the government of a land is in the hands of another nation. The ruling classes often fail to enter into the religious life and sympathies of those whom they are governing. The attitude of Pilate toward the Sanhedrin when they sought to gain his permission for the crucifying of Christ and the attitude of Festus in seeking the advice of King Agrippa to help him in framing a charge under which Paul might be sent to the Roman Empire are cases in point, as was also the attitude of Gallio, the pro-consul of Achaia, mentioned in the eighteenth chapter of Acts, who "cared for none of these things" when the Jews brought before him Sosthenes, the ruler of the synagogue, and sought to make trouble over the teachings of Paul.

The restraints and discretion which the Apostle Paul used are exemplary and afford a striking illustration of what is re- quired in foreign mission fields today of missionaries, especially those working among peoples in subjection to other govern- ments. In many years of foreign mission work in Korea, during which period it was under Japanese rule, again and again I learned that the Japanese officials were quite certain that the American and British missionaries were working there as agents for their home governments, and they consistently refused to believe that these foreigners were there for anything other than some sinister motive. The differences of language and customs all accentuate the difficulty of allaying the suspicions of officials. It is interesting to note the way in which Paul as a patriotic Jew went out of his way to inculcate in the hearts of his friends their Christian duty of allegiance and obedience to the Roman officials who, as he states in Romans 13, were the powers that are ordained of God and were indeed ministers of God, to whom they "must needs be in subjection, not only because of the wrath, but also for conscience' sake. For this cause ye pay tribute also; for they are ministers of God's service, attending continually upon this very thing" (Rom. 13:5,6). When im- morality and sin are denounced, as they must be by every con- scientious servant of Christ, it is always easy for those who are occupying positions of authority to feel that the criticism is being directed against them personally. They have often caused the arrest of the speaker or have forbidden him to preach, on the pretext that he has been speaking against the government and has been inciting the people to rebellion.

In Korea for years the singing of such hymns as "Onward, Christian Soldiers" and "The Son of God Goes Forth to War" was forbidden by the Japanese police; and during the recent years of World War II large portions of the hymn books were blacked out by the censors, as containing sentiments of peace or other matters which might encourage the Christians to lose their militant patriotic attitude and slacken their efforts for the victory of the Japanese forces.

Popular Belief in the Existence of Demons. Demon possession and demon worship were common phenomena in Paul's day. Numerous instances are recorded in the Gospels where the Lord Jesus Christ cast out evil spirits in possession of people, and other cases of demon possession are mentioned in the Book of Acts, including the girl at Philippi who was used by her masters as a fortune teller and who became one of the charter members of the church in that city. In the nineteenth chapter of Acts mention is made of the practice of magical arts in Ephesus, and of the value of the books brought to Paul and burned before him by those who had accepted Jesus Christ as Saviour and Lord. All the phenomena mentioned in the New Testament in regard to demon possession, such as dumb spirits and the tremendous physical power manifested by those who are possessed, even the case of the man of Gadara, whose cast-out spirits went into a herd of swine—all these have been duplicated on the foreign mission field. And as in the Lord's time, so also today, the demons themselves recognize the authority of the Name of Jesus and have been cast out in His Name. J. L. Nevius' *Demonology* contains detailed and accurate accounts of similar more recent incidents which were carefully authenticated.

The Gospel Always Creates Problems

The Lord Himself warned His disciples of this fact in His words, "Think ye that I am come to give peace in the earth? I tell you nay, but rather division; for there shall be from henceforth five in one house divided, three against two, and two against three. They shall be divided, father against son, and son against father; mother against daughter, and daughter against her mother; mother-in-law against her daughter-in-law, and daughter-in-law against her mother-in-law" (Luke 12:51-53). Wherever the gospel goes and enters into the hearts and lives of people in heathen lands, problems and persecution always arise and are expected as the normal thing; for the gospel cuts across every phase of life which is permeated by heathen practices and idolatrous customs. This is as true today as it was in Paul's day. The relation of a Christian to the unbelieving members of his family and clan, his responsibilities toward the communal life of his village, his attitude to the demands of a non-Christian government to engage in practices which violate his conscience, his participation in social and patriotic practices which cut across Christian standards—all these problems have to be faced in every mission field today and require Spirit-given wisdom, grace, and courage, as they did in Apostolic times.

QUESTIONS FOR DISCUSSION

1. Discuss the power of idolatry as revealed in I Corinthians 10:19-20, and what the line of approach of the foreign missionary should be as he discusses this question with: (a) new Christians; and (b) adherents to heathen religions.
2. Study Ephesians 5:22-6:9, discussing all that it emphasizes concerning family relationships and the revolutionary ideas which it introduces as the basis of a Christian home.
3. Discuss the relations of missionaries to government officials, emphasizing the need to spend time and effort in cultivating their friendship and to take special care to avoid giving any offense or to cause misunderstanding.
4. Discuss possible problems which the spread of the gospel may easily create in connection with: (a) home relations (b) social customs; and (c) governmental regulations.

Chapter XVIII

PAULINE MISSIONARY METHODS

THE LIFE and example of Paul as a foreign missionary should be made the subject of careful study by every prospective missionary or student of missions. The fundamental problems, the opposing forces, the essential equipment, the strategic methods, and the promise of victory, are the same today as they were then; and the more thoroughly the present day missionary can have his mind saturated with the Pauline example and method, the better prepared he will be to look for the same sort of startling successes which marked the career of that great apostle.

His Missionary Journeys

In addition to the three great missionary journeys, with which every student of the Book of Acts is familiar, and his journey to Rome as a prisoner, there were certain other travels he had taken before he began his first missionary journey, and also between his first and second Roman imprisonments. All of these involved dangers and hardships of many kinds, to which he refers in II Corinthians, chapter 4, verses 8-11; chapter 6, verses 4-5; and chapter 11, verses 23-28. Many of these experiences and dangers have been duplicated many times in the lives of pioneer missionaries from Paul on down through succeeding years and they are in many cases an integral part of foreign missionary experience. It is noticeable that these journeys were carried on by the Apostle Paul with two main purposes, the same purposes his successors have had.

To Plant Churches. Paul was an intrepid missionary pioneer, whose great desire was, as he states, "Making it my aim so to preach the Gospel, not where Christ was already named, that I might not build upon another man's foundation" (Romans 15:20). The thrill of preaching the gospel in places where the name of Jesus Christ is not known made a great appeal to the Apostle Paul, and has made a similar appeal to many others since. To those to whom God has given the privilege of pioneering, He gives the grace with which to meet the inevitable difficulties and privations, and the courage also to speak the Word with boldness and clarity, so that those hearing for the first time may understand something of the message of God's love. The fearless and clear preaching of the Gospel of the Lord Jesus Christ was the instrument used by the Holy Spirit to win men to Christ in Paul's day (Rom. 1:16, 17; 10:13-18; 15:20, 21), and the same is true in ours, and similar miracles of transformed lives that attended apostolic preaching should be expected today by those whom the Lord has commissioned to go forth as His ambassadors.

To Establish the Christian in the Faith. On his way home from his first missionary journey he returned by way of Lystra and Iconium to Antioch, "Confirming the souls of the disciples, exhorting them to continue in the faith, and that through many tribulations we must enter into the kingdom of God" (Acts 14:22). An effective missionary is one who looks forward to much traveling for both of these purposes—to preach the gospel in hitherto unreached districts in order to establish churches, and then to visit the churches already formed to confirm the believers and to establish them in the faith, assisting and directing in instruction, in discipline, in Christian living and witnessing and in organization. Through this work the affairs of the church can be carried on in an orderly manner and high standards of Christian living maintained; the many problems also which constantly arise in new churches can be met and solved in a way that shall glorify God and shall strengthen the faith and the testimony of the believers. There is a vast difference between the follow-up work practiced by Paul and what goes by the same name today. In Paul's day it was vital instruction and exhortation to confirm and strengthen faith and to establish the Christians in the face of persecution and temptations. His visits to the churches were neither regular nor often and he commended the believer "to God, and to the word of his grace, which is able to build you up, and to give you the inheritance among all them that are sanctified" (Acts 20:32). It was not a case of remaining with them to build a church brick by brick, day after day. It was rather a matter of planting the seed and trusting God to cause it to grow, while as opportunities offered themselves, he, Paul, and others returned to water it and to prune as might be necessary (I Cor. 3:5-8). Some writers go so far as to advocate "no permanent mission stations." Experiences in the foreign mission field, however, indicate that with conditions as they are today in most fields, the ideal method is to establish a permanent home where a number of missionary families can live together, while the men go out and cover wide areas of territory, preaching the gospel and confirming the Christians.

THE GUIDANCE OF THE SPIRIT

Luke does not give us any details as to what method the Holy Spirit used to "forbid" (Acts 16:6) the apostles to go to preach in the Roman Province of Asia, or as to how "the Spirit of Jesus did not suffer them" (Acts 16:7) when they desired to go north into Bithynia, but in any event His guidance was so clear that Paul and Silas had no uncertainty in their own minds as to God's plan for them. As they were waiting in Troas, wondering what God had for them, Paul received his vision of the man from Macedonia, and Luke says, "Straightway we sought to go forth into Macedonia, concluding that God had called us to preach the gospel unto them" (Acts 16:10). Paul had desired to go north and probably east into Bithynia, instead of which he was directed of the Spirit to go north and west over into Macedonia and the continent of Europe, and it is interesting to think of what might have happened and how different world history might have been written, had Paul gone his own way, rather than to the west and Europe.

The more we think of the truths revealed in those passages of Scripture, the more we realize that the whole work and program of foreign missions can succeed only as it is directed by the Holy Spirit. It should remind us also of the great necessity for each missionary daily to commit himself and his work to the Lord in humble submission, so that he may receive the needed guidance from the Holy Spirit as to how he should spend his time and as to where he should first direct his attention in the work of proclaiming the gospel of Christ. The many churches which came into existence as a result of Paul's missionary journeys are adequate testimony to the effectiveness of the way in which he both preached and lived the gospel.

THE RAPIDITY OF HIS SUCCESSES

Rapid Organization. On Paul's first missionary journey it is to be noticed that he founded churches in a number of places, including Iconium and Derbe and Lystra; and on his return trip he visited the churches, *ordaining elders* in each place (Acts

14:21-23). It is to us an astonishing fact that these men were ordained to this holy office within only a few months from the date of their conversion. Whether their conversion was from Judaism or from heathenism the rapidity of their ordination is astonishing. Having organized the churches in this way, Paul left them very much to themselves, under the guidance of these newly appointed officers, who were responsible not only for conducting the meetings but for preaching, for instructing new converts in the faith, and for maintaining the necessary discipline among them.

While Paul was evidently guided by the Holy Spirit in a very definite way in this act of ordination of elders, few missionaries since that time have felt led to follow this example. Whether it has been due to a lack of faith or of courage on the part of the missionaries or to a slower growth on the part of the converts of a later time, it is not for us to say. There is one thing however that is very clear, namely, that in the apostolic age new converts and new churches were very much more quickly left to develop and grow by themselves in direct dependence upon the Holy Spirit, and there was apparently no plan for supporting them financially, or for direct apostolic oversight as is so often true in much of modern missionary work.

Teaching of Doctrine. All of Paul's Epistles in our possession today are full of doctrinal teaching, which proves not only that the great Christian doctrines had fully developed at that early age, but also that Paul had no hesitation in presenting them to the new converts and fully expected them to understand, to assimilate, and to apply them in their daily living.

The Epistles to the Thessalonians were doubtless the first of Paul's letters and were sent to his Christian friends in Thessalonica whom he had won to faith in Christ during his visit there some time before, a visit which had lasted for only a few months before he was driven out of the city by some bigoted Jews. It is of special interest to observe how many of the great doctrines are mentioned in those two brief letters. These include the three Persons of the Trinity, election, sanctification, inspiration, and with particular emphasis, the second coming of Christ, the certainty and the hope of which are closely linked to purity of life in a very practical way. The church of the twentieth century has fallen far from the doctrinal standards and teaching of the Apostolic age, but it is encouraging to know that when and where the doctrines of the gospel are taught today, as they were in Paul's day, to people only recently out of heathenism and savagery, the Holy Spirit enlightens the eyes of their understanding and enables them to comprehend and to make practical application in their daily living. The transformation of their lives is just as startling and profound today as it was in the era of the early church.

Widespread Results. The widespread results of the preaching of Paul were noticeable in various ways. They were seen in the way in which in a comparatively short time churches were established in a number of the strategic centers of the Roman Empire. They were seen in the number of converts won, among whom were men and women of influence, position, and wealth. In his third missionary journey Paul spent most of three years in Ephesus, and we read, "All they that dwelt in Asia heard the word of the Lord" (Acts 19:10). In that three years' period the Word of the Lord evidently spread from the metropolitan city of Ephesus throughout the Roman province of Asia, becoming the topic of conversation in the villages and market places and influencing the lives of a great many. The striking results of Paul's preaching were also seen in the verdicts rendered by his enemies. The city of Ephesus was the center of the worship of the great goddess Diana. She was supposedly the universal mother of all life and symbolized the reproductive power in men and animals and the nourishing power by which the earth gives to man and animals what they need. The worship of this goddess was accompanied by ceremonial prostitution and awful immorality. The teaching of Paul took such a hold on the minds of the people that the livelihood of the silversmiths was greatly affected. For these men made their living from the sale of small silver shrines which were set in homes as objects of worship or carried on the person as charms. But the popular demand for these shrines had so dropped that the silversmiths said, "Almost throughout all Asia, this Paul hath persuaded and turned away much people . . . and not only is there danger that this our trade come into disrepute; but also that the temple of the great goddess Diana be made of no account, and that she should even be deposed from her magnificence, whom all Asia and the world worshippeth" (Acts 19:26-27). At Thessalonica also the charge was made, "These that have turned the world upside down are come hither also" (Acts 17:6).

Simple Organization. Little did the twelve apostles dream of the way in which church organization would develop in the movement which the Holy Spirit used them to inaugurate the years immediately following the ascension of the Lord. It is evident that they had not thought out in advance any of the elaborate schemes of church government which have since developed. The pressure of conditions in those churches led the apostles under the guidance of the Holy Spirit to take steps to meet the needs.

Deacons (Acts 6). The first step in church organization recorded is that found in Acts 6, the election of the seven deacons. They were chosen by the people at the suggestion of the apostles to take care of the church benevolences. From its earliest history the church took upon itself the responsibility of providing for its needy members, and the large number of widows in Jerusalem who had come into the church provided a field demanding special attention. The apostles felt that should they take care of this responsibility, they would be drawn away from their primary duty of prayer and the ministry of the Word, and so at their suggestion, men "full of the Holy Spirit and wisdom" were appointed to take care of the distribution of the funds received, on behalf of the widows and others in need. This particular form of office, under one name or another, has ever since then existed in almost every branch of the Christian church.

Elders. Later on, with the growth and development of the church, the office of elders (or bishops) was instituted. Paul in his first letter to Timothy and in his Epistle to Titus speaks of the qualifications for and duties of this office. The office had a twofold responsibility: one in connection with the ministry of the Word, or teaching, and the other with discipline, or ruling. It is evident from Paul's Epistles that discipline occupied a far larger place in the life of the apostolic church than it does in the life of the church today, and the same thing is true in most mission fields where conditions far more closely approximate those of the early Christian era where people are lately out of heathenism and are meeting tremendous pressure and persecution from their families and heathen friends. Lapses into gross sins and even into idolatrous practices are tragically easy, and it has proved very helpful to exercise discipline in such cases so as to maintain high standards of Christian living and church membership.

QUESTIONS FOR DISCUSSION

1. Discuss the main purposes of Paul's great missionary journeys, pointing out their mutual relationship and their practical importance today.
2. Look up all passages in Acts and the Pauline Epistles indicating the Holy Spirit's guidance and direction in the plan of Paul's preaching.
3. Discuss the place of the Holy Spirit in church organization, both in regard to the offices and to the way in which the officers are appointed or elected to them.
4. Discuss the place of doctrinal instruction as an important part of the work of a foreign missionary, noting the relationship between doctrine and life as pointed out by Paul.

CHAPTER XIX

THE STANDARDS OF THE EARLY CHURCH

HIGH STANDARDS

A CAREFUL reading of the New Testament epistles reveals the standards required both for the officers and for the members of the churches in those days. It makes clear how very far the standards of the church in the present day have fallen from that high level of the apostolic era. The high standards of the New Testament church give clear indication as to how the Holy Spirit led His servants in the early days, as they were setting the foundations for a new world-wide organization. Foreign missionaries today do well when they seek to apply the same standards to the young churches in whose planting they have a part in the lands to which God has called them.

Standards for Elders (Tit. 1:5-9; I Tim. 3:1-7). These two passages clearly state the requirements for those who were to be appointed or elected as elders or leaders of the churches. They were to be men of exemplary character, blameless in reputation both in their homes and in their communities, men not easily aroused to anger or violence in word or action, and men who were familiar with the Scriptures and the doctrine so as to be able to teach and preach and take charge of the services.

Standards for Deacons (Acts 6:3; I Tim. 3:8-10). The standards for deacons who were chosen to administer the benevolence funds of the church were likewise very high. They were to be men of good report, Spirit-filled, and possessing wisdom and judgment and tact. These were deemed very necessary for the proper discharge of the specific duties and responsibilities committed to them. They, too, were to be men of dignity and of experience who were trusted by their associates.

Standards for Members. The standards for church members, as laid down in the New Testament, were also high. It is interesting to notice the following phases of their activities which are covered in various passages of the New Testament.

1. Family Relations (Eph. 5:22-6:9). The unit of society

in God's sight is the family. Therefore Paul takes special care
in several of his epistles, notably in the Epistle to the Ephesians,
to outline the family relationships which must be guarded and
preserved and the high standards which must be maintained, if
that family as a unit is to be one that will please God. He
takes up the three relationships of husbands and wives, parents
and children, and masters and slaves. In those days slaves
formed a part of many of the households and to them was
often given the responsibility of the teaching and training and
care of the younger children; thus they are included as members
of the family.

2. Generous Giving (II Cor. 8:1-5). Throughout the New
Testament the relationship between the various members of
the church and the mutual responsibilities which they must
meet are mentioned often. The apostle Paul placed great
emphasis upon offerings for the poor saints in Jerusalem who
were suffering as the result of a severe famine. This loving care
upon the part of the members one for another is not only an
example and witness to those without the church and a manifestation of the love of Christ in the hearts of God's people, but
as nothing else it binds together the members of the church
and builds up a sense of the unity of all who are in Christ.

3. Thoughtfulness and Courtesy (Acts 15:19-21). At the
first great apostolic conference in Jerusalem, which was called
to deal with the question of what was necessary for Gentile
Christians to be received into the church and to receive salvation,
the decision reached forms an excellent example of Christian
thoughfulness and courtesy. In that decision, while it was made
clear that the Gentile Christians would not be compelled to
observe the intricate Mosaic ritual and receive circumcision as
a sign that they were under obligation to keep the law, nevertheless they were charged with refraining from certain practices
which would needlessly cause offense to the Jewish members.
Paul in his letters again and again also gives examples of
similar Christian courtesy and thoughtfulness in the highest
sense.

4. Foods Sacrificed to Idols (I Cor. 8:1-13; 10:32,33; Rom.
14:1-4). The question as to whether Christians should partake
of food, part of which had already been presented to idols, was
a very live one in the early church—just as it is today in that
and similar forms in many mission fields. Paul clearly set
down the standard which has been followed ever since; it must

be followed if the churches are to maintain the witness among the heathen peoples where they have been established.

5. Forgiveness (Philemon). The whole Epistle to Philemon is a beautiful example not only of Christian courtesy on the part of Paul, but an exhortation to fulfill the Christian duty of forgiveness on the part of Philemon to his runaway slave Onesimus, who had gone to Rome and had there come in contact with Paul and had been saved. Although according to Roman law, Philemon possessed the right to have his runaway slave flogged to death, Onesimus was now being sent back to his former master, with the request from Paul that he be received, "no longer as a bondservant, but more than a bondservant, a brother beloved, especially to me, but now much rather to thee, both in the flesh and in the Lord."

6. Clean Language. Profanity and the blaspheming of God's name is a sin which is confined mainly to so-called Christian countries, although there is in heathen lands much vileness in ordinary conversation (Eph. 5:3-6). Paul applied clean standards of Christian living not merely to conduct but also to thoughts in conversation and in vocabulary.

7. Equal Treatment to Church Members (Jas. 2:1-4). The Apostle James, in his Epistle, gives special instruction that the same treatment be given to a poor man as to one of wealth and means. Money and position were not to be allowed to cause preference and all members were to be dealt with on a common basis of their relationship in and through the Lord Jesus Christ.

8. Persecution (Phil. 1:28-30; I Pet. 2:20-24; I Pet. 4:12-19). Persecution was the normal lot and was to be expected by every Christian in those days. It is hard for many to realize that through the centuries and even now throughout the world persecution has been the lot of the great majority of true believers. Even today, with the exception of the English-speaking and the Scandinavian countries, practically everywhere throughout the world, to make a public and a sincere profession of faith in Jesus Christ means persecution of one kind or another. The apostles make it plain that such treatment was in no way to be considered as unexpected. On the contrary, persecution was to be regarded as a privilege, for it is under persecution particularly that the Christians find their greatest opportunities of manifesting the love and the grace, the courage and the power which come from the Holy Spirit, and thereby reveal to their persecutors something of the tremendous transformation which

has come into their lives as the result of knowing Christ. It is not an uncommon remark on the part of Christians in churches in the mission fields that, "It is time we had another persecution to warm us up, for we are getting cold in the faith." I often reminded my Korean brethren that persecution is like a lens which focuses the attention of the world upon a believer and enables the world to see the sustaining power and the grace of the Lord, which are revealed then as at no other time, in the life of His servant.

9. Relation to Officials (Rom. 13:1-10; Tit. 3:1; I Pet. 2:13-17). The relation to officials was a subject to which both Paul and Peter referred in their epistles. Suspicion on the part of the officials is still one of the problems which nearly every Christian has to face in the mission field. It must have been a peculiarly acute problem in Paul's day when the people to whom he was speaking were a part of the Roman Empire, though comparatively few of them were Romans themselves but were subject peoples. Faith in Jesus Christ nearly always seems to bring with it a renewed love for country, and a new stirring of patriotic feelings may very easily lead to problems with the officials unless directed by the Holy Spirit. Paul as a patriotic Jew must have found it very difficult to exhort his readers to pray for the Roman officials, and to regard them as ministers of God, appointed by Him for their own good. Those officials were often proud and overbearing, far more concerned with their own position and comfort than with the good of the people they were ruling, and yet that is just what Paul is saying in his Epistle to the Romans, and it is along that line that missionaries have often to exhort and counsel with the Christians, especially those living in a country under the domination of European or a foreign Oriental power.

10. Lawsuits (I Cor. 6:1-11). In this passage the Apostle Paul distinctly charges the members of the church at Corinth, when they have difficulties among themselves, not to engage in lawsuits before heathen officials, but to settle the matters among themselves as Christians. Especially in Korea and Africa has this been carried out to a remarkable degree. There the church sessions act as arbiters when quarrels or disputes arise among church members and other Christians, and as a result it is an almost unheard of thing for two Christians to be found involved in a lawsuit against each other.

11. Finances. The New Testament is silent in regard to

financial questions connected with the support and carrying on of church work. No mention is made of salaries for missionaries such as those who travelled with the Apostle Paul on his journeys, or for workers in the newly established churches, although apparently from his words in his First Epistle to Timothy, the custom of paying salaries to ministers had already been started (I Tim. 5:17-18). Neither is anything ever said about raising money for church buildings; in fact, no mention is made in the New Testament of any church building. The churches referred to in the New Testament met in private homes. As the numbers grew and those dwelling houses or the rooms available became inadequate to accommodate the numbers, doubtless buildings were rented or erected and church buildings as such then naturally came into existence.

QUESTIONS FOR DISCUSSION

1. How soon should New Testament standards be applied to newly established churches? Are Pauline standards too strict for today?
2. Discuss the witness of the Christian home as outlined in Ephesians 5:22-6:9 and in the parallel passage in Colossians, and the power of its testimony and among peoples where "home" is a word almost untranslatable.
3. Discuss the results of persecution upon the spiritual life of a church. If it is to be expected as a normal experience in the lives of most Christians, how are they to be encouraged and be prepared to meet it?
4. Look up all references to church funds and finances in the New Testament and seek to discover what principles are laid down concerning them.

CHAPTER XX

PAULINE PRINCIPLES FOR PLANTING
AN INDIGENOUS CHURCH

A S we have already seen, the Book of Acts is a textbook for missionary methods. Of the various books that have been written since on the subject, a noteworthy one is Roland Allen's *Missionary Methods—St. Paul's or Ours?* In that book he points out a number of interesting features in the Pauline principles, some of which will be noted in this chapter.

STRATEGIC CENTERS

Paul has rightly been spoken of as a great missionary states-man. His wisdom is well illustrated in the important centers he chose in which to establish the first churches, under the direct leading of the Holy Spirit.

Provinces Rather than Cities. A reading of Acts 16:9, 10; 18:5; 19:22, and other passages, will reveal the fact that in Paul's thinking it was provinces rather than cities which occupied his attention. This in turn leads us to another important point.

Centers of Christian Life Were Self-Propagating (Acts 19:9, 10). Paul realized that when the power and presence of the Holy Spirit had been planted in the lives of a small group of believers, they themselves would undertake the responsibility of passing the Word along to others, both by their words and their example. In each heathen country a group of Christians, however small, very soon became objects of curiosity and subjects of conversation among their neighbours, because of the great changes manifested in their conduct, their conversation, and their outlook. Paul was depending upon that type of spreading of the news and upon the power of the Holy Spirit to use it for the future enlarging of the work. By the establishing of a church in a strategic center he realized that the gospel would in the course of time naturally be proclaimed throughout the district.

Until the church takes root and becomes a part of the country and people among whom it is established, it is "foreign." As such it is subject to anti-foreign suspicion and opposition and its continued existence is both uncertain and precarious. The criticism has often been leveled at churches in foreign mission fields by the governments of their own countries that they are too much under the domination of foreigners. The church in Ethiopia is one of the most outstanding examples of what can take place when the church is put on its own. At the time of the Italian invasion when all Protestant missionaries had to leave, in one district there was a church of about seventy members. Some five years later, when the missionaries returned, as they supposed, to pick up a few broken pieces, they found over 60,000 Christians in the area formerly occupied by seventy. They were organized into self-supporting, self-governing, and self-propagating churches without any help whatever from a foreign missionary. In spite of persecution from Roman Catholic officials and priests, the work had far exceeded all expectations. Similar reports come from parts of China, where during the Japanese occupation the foreign missionaries had to leave, and where the church, even though it was suddenly forced to depend upon its own resources, with the help of God made surprising progress. Two mission fields where this method of church self-propagation has been most consistently followed are in Korea and in the French Cameroun in Africa. In both these fields the work has been phenomenally successful and rapid in its growth, and the results have proved the high value of this plan.

Churches Established in Influential Cities. The Apostle Paul planted churches in cities which were strategic centers. He did this in order to influence a large area of surrounding country. As Roland Allen points out, a study of the Book of Acts will show that these cities were centers of: (1) Roman administration (law); (2) Greek civilization (language); (3) Jewish influence (religion); and (4) world commerce (leadership in thought). By establishing churches therefore in these centers, the channels of law, of language, of religion, and of leadership in thought would all be made use of to further the proclamation of the gospel.

FINANCES

While church finances are not mentioned very often in the New Testament, nevertheless at least three principles are clearly revealed, principles of which the Apostle Paul made definite use. They are discussed in the following paragraphs.

Paul did not seek financial aid for himself. While it is perfectly true that on several occasions he received gifts from some of the churches which he founded, notably Philippi, these were entirely unsolicited on Paul's part and were the fitting expression of the gratitude and love felt by those whom Paul had won to faith in the Lord through his unremitting activity in the proclamation of the Gospel. Paul realized that for him to seek any financial assistance would be hindrance to his work (I Thess. 2:7-9; II Thess. 3:7-8; II Cor. 11:9-12; Acts 20:33-34). His anxiety to be in no way a burden upon the new converts because of the stumbling block it would so easily become to their growth in faith, was the reason for his supporting himself by his old trade of tent-making. In this connection, however, it should be noted that although Paul's standards for himself were these which we have just noted, at the same time he admitted the legitimacy of a certain class in the church receiving remuneration for their preaching. This is made very clear in I Cor. 9:12; and I Tim. 5:17.

Paul took no financial help to his converts; every church was financially independent from the beginning. The Galatians were exhorted to support their own teachers (Gal. 6:6). Each church was instructed to be responsible for its local benevolences, for the support of the poor among its members. The only occasion recorded on which an offering was taken by the church on behalf of work elsewhere was that in the interests of the poor saints in Jerusalem who were suffering through a famine, for whom Paul took up a collection in many of the churches which he had established. This however was not a normal proceeding and was not to lay down a principle of church finance; it was intended primarily to make plain before all the unity of the members of the church, both Jews and Gentiles.

The third principle observed by the Apostle Paul was that every church should administer its own funds. Paul makes no mention of himself receiving or disbursing any funds, with the exception already referred to of the offering on behalf of the poor brethren in Jerusalem. No central treasury is mentioned to which funds for the churches were sent or which exercised authority in the use of church monies. All these were much later developments in the history of the church. There is a definite place and in many cases a real need for the combining of a portion of the funds from various churches, especially in the interests of carrying on evangelistic and missionary activities of various natures; but the fundamental principle should remain untouched, namely, that every church has the right to administer its own funds and allocates them to the uses it deems best, in accordance with the leading of the Holy Spirit. The application of this principle in foreign mission work would rule out the disbursements of church funds or their allocation to various purposes by the foreign missionary on his own authority, unless he is definitely requested to do so by the churches themselves.

TRAINING OF CONVERTS

The constant references to "tradition" and "the faith" show that at the time of writing the Pauline epistles a definite body of Christian doctrine had grown up which was recognized as a necessary subject of instruction to the new converts (II Thess. 2:15; 3:6; I Cor. 11:2; I Tim. 6:20-21; II Tim. 1:13; 2:2; 3:14; Titus 1:9). An examination of the doctrines referred to makes it clear that they included those of the three Persons of the Trinity and the specific work of each, the teaching of the plan of Salvation, the reading and the teaching of the Old Testament, the Resurrection of the Lord, its evidence and its significance, and the meaning and administration of baptism and of the Lord's Supper.

RESPONSIBILITY FOR SELF-GOVERNMENT

One of the startling things noted in reading the Book of Acts is the way in which the churches were thrown upon their own responsibility for self-government and self-instruction very soon after they were started. The visits made to the newly established churches by Paul and the other apostles were only occasional and it is clear that the local churches were taught from the beginning not to be dependent on the apostles but to meet their own problems by themselves under the guidance of the Holy Spirit. The apostolic conference which met in Jerusalem, as recorded in the 15th chapter of Acts, decided questions of interest to all, in regard to what was necessary to require of Gentile converts who desired to enter the church. The individual churches however were thrown upon their own responsibility to manage their own affairs almost immediately after their beginning. On his first missionary journey Paul preached in Lystra for not more than six months, and on his return to Antioch he ordained elders and did not revisit those churches for nearly two years. It seems clear that on his first visit to

Thessalonica he could not have stayed there for more than five or six months and apparently did not visit the place again for over five years, but the church there was recognized as on a par with the other churches established elsewhere. The same thing is true in regard to his visit to Corinth, where he spent a year and a half on his first visit but did not visit them again for three or four years. The more we think of the significance of these statements, the more we realize how very far common modern missionary practice has departed from the methods of Saint Paul.

Qualifications for Church Officers

Although in the case of Titus it was left to him in Crete to appoint the elders in every city it is also clear that soon after beginning each congregation had a share in the choice of the men from among themselves, who should be their church officers. In the pastoral epistles, also, the Apostle Paul gives clear instructions as to the qualifications of the men who should be chosen for these holy offices. While nothing is said of any qualifications of special education or training, he makes it clear that they should be of high moral character, men of administrative ability, as evidenced by the way in which they ruled their own families and disciplined their own children. They were also to be men well thought of in the community, whose business and social life had won the confidence and respect of outsiders as well as of Christians.

Discipline

Paul makes it clear that discipline was to be administered to those whose conduct had departed from the true faith and who had fallen into grievous sin. I Corinthians 5:5 speaks of judicial action on the part of the church in regard to one of their own members who was guilty of gross immorality. I Timothy 1:20 speaks of Hymenaeus and Alexander, whom Paul "delivered unto Satan, that they might be taught not to blaspheme." This was an act of judicial severity because of grievous sin. II Corinthians 2:6-10 speaks of the administration of punishment and subsequent restoration to full membership. Experience in the foreign mission field has shown that discipline when properly administered has a tremendous influence in maintaining a high standard of Christian living among the members, and in creating standards of Christian living which are recognized not only by the Christians themselves, but are understood by unbelievers as being characteristic of and necessary to a truly Christian life.

"The Church in the House"

It has already been mentioned that there is no reference in the New Testament to church buildings or property. The normal place for a church to begin was in the home of the first believers. As the membership grew so that it was impossible to conveniently entertain them in the home, it stands to reason that through their own efforts they bought or built structures which were used for church buildings. Nowadays the reverse is often the case, a building is rented or erected with foreign funds, looking forward to the establishment of a church.

I shall never forget a conversation reported to me when I was in Manchuria in an early exploratory trip. A Korean colporteur who was travelling with me dropped behind and got into conversation with a young Chinese. I later asked him what they had been talking about, and he said, "Why, of course, I preached Christ to him." On being asked what the response was, he told me that the young man to whom he had been speaking was interested but explained that he must not be expected to believe until after the death of his parents, for they were looking to him to offer sacrifices to their spirits. Then he went on to say, "When I believe, I want to believe in an Eastern doctrine and not a Western one. In the town in which I live a foreign missionary has rented a building and pays the salary of an evangelist to come and hold services. As a result, of course, the whole thing is a foreign doctrine. What I believe, I want to believe the way you Korean Christians do, for we have watched you coming up into this country. When a group of you Christians come, almost before you have finished building your own homes, you put up your church building and have your services there on Sundays and on Wednesday evenings and carry on quite independently of any foreign money or foreign missionary. That is an Eastern doctrine and that is the kind in which I want to believe."

To that young man, as doubtless to many others, the fact that the building rented for worship was paid for by foreign funds and the support of the evangelist himself came from the same source, created a real barrier in his mind. When, as has often been the case, the first church buildings erected have been put up in the Western type of architecture and are entirely unlike anything with which the people are familiar, it only accentuates the "foreign" nature of the doctrine. In more recent years when racial and national self-consciousness has risen to such a high degree almost everywhere, to abandon the age-old heritage of religious beliefs in favour of Western modes of thought and religion seems to many to be unpatriotic. Special care must therefore be taken by the foreign missionary to introduce just as little as possible of "foreign atmosphere" and to present the gospel in its universal aspects, enabling the people themselves to make it their own just as rapidly and naturally as possible.

QUESTIONS FOR DISCUSSION

1. Discuss three principles used by the Apostle Paul, which are evident in his choice of strategic centers for the establishing of churches. Will these apply today as then?
2. Discuss three principles mentioned in connection with church finances as laid down in Acts in their bearing today on financial policies in foreign mission work and on the handling of national church funds by foreign missionaries.
3. Discuss the emphasis which should be placed today upon the teaching of doctrinal standards to young converts.
4. Discuss why missionaries should not be content to do as little teaching of doctrinal standards on the mission field as is usually done in the home churches.
5. Should missions have a settled policy concerning renting buildings or erecting churches with "foreign" funds? Does the Scriptural policy of starting a church "in the house" still apply?

CHAPTER XXI

THE MAGNITUDE OF THE MISSIONARY TASK

A S CAN BE SEEN from a study of the Book of Acts and will be pointed out in later chapters, the methods used by the apostles under the leadership of the Holy Spirit were those which led to the planting of churches on an indigenous basis from their very beginning. This in itself is a very strong reason for the mission work today to be carried on along the same general lines.

A second very cogent argument for the establishment of the indigenous church lies in the enormity of the task which faces the church throughout the world today. This can be regarded from four different phases:

THE VAST INCREASE IN THE HEATHEN POPULATION IN THE WORLD

With the spread of civilizing forces and sanitary methods under more enlightened governments, the heathen population of practically all mission fields has gone up by leaps and bounds, so that there are today very many more unreached heathen than there were in the time of our Lord when He gave His command to the disciples, "To go into all the world and preach the gospel." While it is true that in Europe and in China the ravages and bloodshed of the World Wars carried off millions of the population, nevertheless the rise in the birth rates has already more than made up for the losses, and the high birth rate in almost all mission lands has caused an increase in population out of all proportion to the efforts put forth by the churches through the various missionary societies.

THE UNREACHED MILLIONS IN UNOCCUPIED FIELDS

Statistics on this matter are of course somewhat uncertain, but well-informed statisticians have based the numbers of the unreached millions as follows: Countries in which the gospel has never been preached: Part of Asia—35,000,000; part of Africa—50,000,000; part of South America—20,000,000; or a total of 105,000,000. To this number should be added the unreached populations in the countries now entered and partially occupied, another 700,000,000, a great many of whom have never yet heard the name of the Lord Jesus Christ.

THE SMALLNESS OF MISSIONARY FORCES

The total missionary personnel at its highest figure numbered about 35,000. Shortly before the outbreak of the Second World War the missionary force throughout the world numbered approximately 27,480; since then the number has been greatly decreased. Many were forced to leave on account of war conditions and even yet have not been able to return to their fields. Of these a very large portion will never return because of changed conditions in the mission fields and due to their own age and health. In addition to this, there has been a definite decline in interest in missions in the home churches. Vast sums are being spent today in church building programs, and during this reconstruction period large sums are being raised for restoring at least some of the churches and buildings destroyed by war, not only in the mission fields themselves but also in a considerable part of devastated Europe. Young men and women who otherwise would probably have gone to foreign mission fields are now being diverted to Europe, which in itself has become, as a result of the War, a vast mission field of desperate need and importance.

FINANCIAL LIMITATIONS

In the face of the colossal task confronting the church, both in Europe and in foreign mission lands, there has been a steady decrease in the income of many of the foreign missionary societies and boards. In the Anglo-Saxon countries, which have hitherto been the main supporters of foreign mission work, the high cost of living and increased taxes due to the tremendous expense of the War, have made it all the more difficult to raise large sums for the mission enterprise. In addition, during the last two decades many, if not most, of the large givers have passed away and their places have not been taken by others. In many sections of the church a lack of confidence in the denominational mission boards and in the type of work they are doing has arisen and has naturally resulted in a decrease in the giving of their members. These conditions have greatly lessened the amounts available for missionaries to open up pioneer work in new territories.

The Foreign Missionary

Another very strong argument for the establishment of indigenous churches lies in the nature of the foreign missionary himself. It is the studied opinion and conviction of a great majority of those who have had experience in foreign mission work that at best the average foreign missionary himself is but an expensive and only partially efficient stop-gap, or at least should develop the habit of regarding himself as such, until the indigenous church has been established. This is my conviction after nearly a quarter of a century of work in Korea.

His Comparative Inefficiency. In making a statement of this kind, care has to be taken to see that false impressions are not made and that no injustice is done to that splendid body of consecrated men and women who have been tremendously effective ambassadors of Jesus Christ, as they have spread the gospel in many lands. First, be it said that the term "inefficiency" does in no sense apply to the work or the methods used or the character of the instruction given. Nearly every foreign missionary after a few years becomes a specialist in his own line of work, and his line is essentially that of an organizer and partial director in the carrying out of a great program of evangelization and the establishment of an indigenous church. In these items in nearly every case the foreign missionary is far superior to the national Christians and leaders with whom he is called upon to work; but as a general thing, in personal evangelism he is inferior in effectiveness to the nationals among whom he is working.

Whether in reference to accent, tone, grammar, or idioms, only the very exceptional missionary ever reaches the place where he "talks like a native." A foreign missionary will almost always necessarily be a "foreigner" in the land to which he has been sent—in his clothes, his appearance, his accent, his customs, his viewpoints, and his background. While in recent years Western style clothes have become a familiar sight in almost every land, almost any missionary who has had experience in pioneer work can tell amusing stories from his own experience of feeling encouraged at the apparent rapt attention on the part of some of his listeners to what he was saying. Then to his disillusionment later on he learns their minds in reality were concerned not with the subject matter of his talk but with the strangeness of his clothes, the color of his hair, his strange features, and similar matters. I have been interrupted by my listeners, eager to know, not of the truth of the gospel of which I was speaking, but whether the hair on my wrists meant that my whole body was similarly covered, or how it was possible for me to see from my "deep set" eyes.

The methods and ideals of the foreign missionary will always set him apart from those among whom he is working. As an outsider, a missionary rarely if ever is regarded by those to whom he is speaking as one who has the right to criticize or to make disparaging remarks on their superstitious native customs, or on the hypocrisy and deceitfulness of the sorcerers and priests. Although a foreigner would never dare to make fun of these in public, I have often seen national Christian workers do so to the great enjoyment and approval of the listening crowds. The same is true also in exercising discipline among church members; the average foreign missionary would rarely find it wise to exercise discipline by as severe methods as many of the national leaders use and use regularly without fear of criticism.

A foreigner when entering an unevangelized village for the first time usually will have to spend days or possibly weeks before he can really enter into the life of the people and can preach the gospel to them in an effective way, even though he is familiar with the language and many of their customs. One of their own people can start in after thirty minutes and present Jesus Christ from his own experience and viewpoint, which will often be almost exactly identical with those to whom he is speaking. Again, let me repeat that the inefficiency on the part of the foreign missionary lies in no sense in his lack of consecration or intelligence or training. It lies simply in the fact that he is a "foreigner" and will always remain such. His usefulness in certain phases is thereby enhanced in many ways, but when it comes to the real pioneer work of personal evangelism, to be done effectively and rapidly it must be carried on by the nationals themselves.

His Expense. The foreign missionary is also a very expensive agent from almost any viewpoint. In addition to his salary, there are other very necessary expenses, including housing, medical care, travel expense, furloughs, and similar items, for which provision has to be made. All these add up to a tremendous sum in comparison with the expense involved in the support of national workers. In some mission fields a few missionaries have tried "going native," by living in native houses, wearing native dress, living on native food, and as far as possible identifying themselves with the people among whom they live. Probably God does occasionally call a few of His people to carry on their work in that way, but it is the general consensus of opinion of those who are in a position to know best that going to that length is dangerous from the point of view of health; there is a great question also as to whether the influence of the particular missionary is enhanced thereby. The missionary is not a permanent but only a temporary measure or bridge until an indigenous church has been planted, which is able to carry on its own work and support itself. It is highly important that each missionary going out, from the very beginning, has this view of himself and his work. As has been said, the missionary's objective is "to work himself out of a job," that is, to make himself no longer necessary. The sooner he reaches that state the sooner he has the satisfaction of knowing that he has completed his particular task in that particular territory.

When I was a junior missionary the late Dr. Samuel A. Moffett of Korea pointed out to me in a conversation this truth which I shall never forget: "A good foreign missionary should never look forward to having the satisfaction of doing his job perfectly." I was surprised and on asking the reason why, he went on to explain to me, "You are here to help in the establishment of a church. It is not however your church; it is the Korean church. Just as soon therefore as you find a Korean who can do the work you are doing, even though you know he will not do it as well as you and will make mistakes, nevertheless you should be ready to step out and put him in your place, while you begin something else. The sooner he begins the sooner he will learn to carry on the work of his church."

That should be, I believe, the attitude and the point of view of every missionary. It requires grace and humility to carry it through consistently but there is no question that only as such a viewpoint is maintained can the work be put on an indigenous basis quickly. It is insidiously easy for a missionary to feel that he has been sent by God to do a great piece of work and that therefore his success will be measured by the number of people whom he directs and the number of churches which he builds up. Insensibly he comes to regard himself as a spiritual overlord and one who is indispensable to the establishment and the development of the work in his care. The correct attitude of course is the reverse, that it is the Lord who is planting the church and the Lord who is building up a work largely through the nationals, to whom the responsibility should be given just as soon as possible, while the foreign missionary himself becomes expendable for another new work, with no unnecessary delay.

Its Success

The planting of the indigenous church is the only way to insure growth that is *normal*. By normal, I mean that it grows by itself and is not an artificial organization under the direction of an outsider. It is normal in that it is the natural development growing out of the work of the Holy Spirit in the lives of the people in that country.

Its manner of growth produces a *sturdy* plant—sturdy, in that from the beginning the roots of the new work are developed in a spirit of independence from foreign funds, from foreign direction, and from foreign leadership. At first the growth may seem rather slow; as the work develops, however, speed picks up.

After this stage has been reached, the growth is really *rapid*. For as every Christian becomes in turn a personal worker and evangelist among his own people, the work grows in geometrical progression.

This method makes for a *permanent church*. In these days of world-wide uncertainty, with nationalistic lines being drawn tauter and in some places foreign missionary work becoming more restricted, it is only as the church has become an integral part of its own country, free from foreign support and control, that it can be expected to have a sense of stability and permanence.

QUESTIONS FOR DISCUSSION

1. Discuss the four phases in which the magnitude of the missionary task is considered in this chapter.
2. In what way should a foreign missionary regard himself in relation to the church which he is seeking to establish and what practical effect will this have on his methods of work?
3. In what ways does being "foreigners" detract from the usefulness and effectiveness of a missionary and in what ways may it be a distinct advantage?
4. Discuss the various characteristics mentioned of a church which is established on the indigenous basis and compare them with those of a church established on what formerly was the usual plan.

CHAPTER XXII

ADMINISTRATIVE PROBLEMS

E VEN A SURVEY of this kind would not be complete without at least a brief mention of the following three factors in missionary work, and their relationships to each other. These are: the home board or home committee, the field mission, and the field church. Each has its own particular sphere of work and its own responsibilities, and these in turn must be clearly understood and differentiated if the work is to be carried out with effective and permanent results. Added to the administrative problems of these units there may also be the problem of the transfer of authority.

THE BOARD OR HOME COMMITTEE

The responsibilities and duties of the home board or home committee include among others the following important matters.

Appointment of Missionaries. The careful examination and passing upon qualifications of missionary candidates is a question of increasing importance. The responsibilities and burdens of missionary life demand men and women who are physically able to carry on under conditions which would break down those of weaker physical natures. They should be men and women of poise and ability to live with others without undue friction. They should also be men and women thoroughly consecrated to the Lord for His service and with a background of Bible knowledge and Christian experience and training for their work that will render them efficient as ambassadors of the Lord Jesus. It goes without saying that the better trained a person is the more effective his or her work will be on the foreign field. It is the responsibility of the board or the home committee to decide upon the standards and qualifications required of the candidates they appoint. These qualifications may vary considerably according to the climate, the cultural state, and the degree of civilization of those to whom they will be sent, as well as the particular type of work to which they will be assigned. In recent years, with the new methods of screening applicants, great advances have been made and on the whole much greater care is now being taken in the selection of missionary candidates. This has resulted in fewer misfits and fewer breakdowns, physical or nervous, among those who have been sent.

Gathering and Transmission of Funds to the Mission Field. Some boards or missions now require their missionary candidates before going out to secure their support by creating interest among churches or individuals who would underwrite their expenses; nevertheless, the responsibility of receiving those funds and sending them out to the field must of necessity remain with the home committee or board.

Cultivation of Interest among the Home Constituency. Everyone realizes that the progress and success, particularly of mission work on the field, will depend very largely upon the interest and the prayers of the home constituency. This interest must be carefully cultivated so that the people will be intelligent in their praying; this can only be done by a well-worked out plan for publicity and for gathering the items of news and importance from the mission field and sending them back to those who are interested in the homeland. Many mission boards could well afford to spend greater effort and more careful thoughts on this very important part of their work; though an increased emphasis doubtless means an additional expense, it would be well warranted and more than justified by the results.

Review and Control of Policies and Program of the Mission. The home boards or committees should exercise the authority of review and control in regard to the policies and methods of the work carried on by the missionaries in the field. It is therefore their responsibility to keep themselves thoroughly familiar with the needs of the field and with its special problems. This should include an understanding of the policies in use by the missionaries and a readiness to suggest changes where they feel such should be made in the better interests of the work. It is also their responsibility to see that the proper use is made of the budget and that the various items of expenditure are kept in proper proportion.

Where missions have started out on what we have been speaking of as the old-line policy of establishing churches under foreign missionary leadership and with the use of foreign funds, and a realization has come that a change-over should be made to the indigenous church policy, as outlined in the previous chapters, then appropriate action by the home committee will be of tremendous help. Regardless of where the decision originated, whether in the mission on the field or in the home committee, the home committee should give official instructions in regard to the carrying out of that policy. In this way the burden for making the necessary changes will rest not upon the individual missionaries or mission concerned but upon the headquarters in the home base. When these changes are made and funds cut down, for a while at least, it is very easy for the national Christians to feel hurt and take the position that discontinuance of funds is a sign that the missionaries themselves are losing interest or at least sympathy for their co-laborers. If the missionaries therefore are able to say that the responsibility for the decision rests with the committee in the homeland, it takes a heavy burden from their shoulders and insures a better relationship with the national Christians concerned.

All major decisions on basic policies are made and administered by the home board or committee. Among them the following three are included.

(1) Length of Furloughs and Length of Terms of Service of Missionaries: Terms of service will vary in accordance with the climatic and physical conditions in the different mission fields and to a degree upon the particular type of work in which the missionaries are engaged. The length of furlough will also vary to a certain extent in accordance with the number of years spent on the field, but these decisions must be made by the home committee as well as the giving of special permission in case of particular conditions arising through the ill health of missionaries or possibly emergencies in connection with their homes or with members of their families in the home country.

(2) Salaries of Missionaries: This question also should not be decided upon by the missionaries themselves. While they may very properly make recommendations as to the amounts needed, especially in view of sudden rises in the cost of living or de-valuation of currencies, the responsibility for making the final decision must rest with the home board.

(3) Amounts of Funds used for Mission Work: Experience has shown that a very careful distinction should always be kept between the budgets for the missionaries and their families and those used to meet the expenses of carrying on missionary work. Careful estimates should be made in advance by the missionaries on the field as to what will be needed during the following year so that the home committee can have the necessary information

in order to make a careful study as to the funds needed and to make preparation for forwarding them.

THE MISSION

Just as the board or the home committee has its own particular sphere of work or activity, so also the mission on the field has its own special sphere of work and responsibility. Five of these responsibilities are now discussed.

Assignment of Missionaries. The mission, being on the field of labor and having first-hand acquaintance with conditions and needs, usually has the authority to decide upon the assignment of its workers so that the most efficient use can be made of them. This will include not only the assignment of new workers but also the best disposition to be made of the older and more experienced ones. In accordance with conditions on the field, the mission will make the decisions as to the number of workers to be located in each station and also from time to time, as necessity arises, it must make decisions to solve personal questions of incompatability between workers who may be located in the same station. This may necessitate the transfer of one or more.

Apportionment of Work to Missionaries. The work of each missionary should be a matter of direct assignment by the mission so that each member is responsible in turn to the mission as a whole for the type and amount of work which he or she undertakes. This plan has proved valuable from various points of view; it sets standards for the work of each individual missionary and it does a great deal to insure uniformity of method and policy throughout the mission field. It also avoids overlapping of work and it safeguards against the omission of making provision for special needs.

Decisions Concerning Policies and Methods of Work. It is highly necessary that a uniform policy of work and methods be maintained throughout the entire work of any given mission field. Such a condition will make for solidarity in principles and methods and will do much to avoid misunderstandings and confusion, especially between missionaries and national Christians, as the latter move from one district to another. Having visited mission fields where uniform policies had not been insisted upon and where, as in the time of the Judges, "Every man did that which was right in his own eyes," I have personally witnessed the confusion and lack of cohesion which existed in the mission itself and also in the local church which was being established in that field. When a mission policy has been definitely worked out and is uniformly upheld, it helps to solve many problems dealing with the national Christians on matters of finances as well as on moral and spiritual standards. It also helps to save the inexperienced individual missionary from making questionable decisions, by thus having precedents and rules which experience has shown to be wise.

Distribution and Use of Mission Funds. There is a great need for careful and well-thought-out rules and policies in regard to the use of mission funds and to their distribution, both among the various mission stations and missionaries and also among the various types of work carried on. It is highly essential that a strict system of auditing accounts of all mission monies should be put into effect in order that the mission as a whole may have complete knowledge at any time as to the expenditure of all its funds, even to details, so that it may be in a position to find the most efficient method of distribution and the best method of use in each department.

Decisions Regarding the Relationship of the Mission to the National Church or Churches. A source of an acute problem arising these days between missions or missionaries and national churches is that of reciprocal relationships and the delegation of authority. In a good many mission fields there is an increasing insistence on the part of national churches that the authority which has been heretofore exercised by the foreign missionaries be delegated to the church and that the responsibility of making important decisions in regard to the work and in certain places even in regard to the location and assignment of missionaries be turned over to the national churches. Concerning this question, two principles should be borne in mind: First, it is always wise for the missionaries to be so forward looking in their attitude that they will be ready to turn over authority to the national church before a request is made for it. Such an attitude will do much toward avoiding anti-foreign feeling and similar complicated difficulties. The other principle is that when it comes to turning over authority to national churches, it should be carried out as a uniform policy throughout the whole mission, and not be left to the will of individual missionaries so that some will move ahead while others will maintain the *status quo.* The need for uniformity in regard to making such changes is very great and should be dictated by the majority vote of the mission concerned.

The Church

The third factor in mission administration, as we have seen, is the church, and great care should be taken from the start that neither the mission nor individual missionaries should ever infringe upon the rights and responsibilities of the church. It must always be kept in mind that the mission in its nature and activities is and always will be a "foreign" institution, while the church should be from the very moment of its inception an indigenous organization. As a result its responsibility should be recognized from the start, along the following lines:

Appointment of Its Officers. When for the very first time a small group of new believers gather together and undertake to conduct their own services and begin their corporate life as a church, in the nature of the case, the foreign missionary in charge will probably have to designate certain ones as leaders or temporary officers. However, after a year has elapsed, or just as soon as some of the believers have been baptized and have thereby become full members, they should be instructed in their responsibilities as such, should be taught without delay to make use of their privileges, and in a prayerful way, should formally elect the officers and leaders of their group. In this way from the very beginning they enjoy the self-respect which exercising the rights and privileges of church membership brings with it.

Administration of Its Funds. Each local church from its inception should be taught its inalienable right to administer its own funds. It is unnecessary to speak of the importance of wise and faithful guidance in regard to this matter from the missionary. The new believers, particularly those who have been elected or appointed to take charge of the finances, however small the funds may be, should be taught the rudiments of keeping simple accounts and of making regular reports to the other members as to the amounts received and the manner in which they have been disbursed. The officers to whom such authority has been delegated should discuss the whole plan with the members so as to give every one a clear understanding of how the church's finances are handled and in what ways they can be the most effectively used to the glory of God and to the building up of the church, both locally and elsewhere.

The Plan of Organization. In a pioneer field after a number

of groups have been established, in consultation with representatives duly appointed for each one, the whole plan of organization should be freely discussed and the right of making the
final decision should rest with the local believers. In these early
stages the foreign missionaries themselves will exercise the right
to vote, inasmuch as for the time being at least they will form
an integral part of the newly organized church, and will be
anxious to identify themselves with it in its development and
progress. As the work goes forward, amendments and changes
of various kinds in the plan of organization will be found advisable, and these may be made on the recommendation of either
the missionary or the church members, but the right of decision
must always and inevitably rest with the church.

Methods and Policies of the Work. All methods and policies
of conducting the business of the church must be decided by
the church itself. It is a temptation for the foreign missionary,
especially in the early stages, to feel that the authority for making
changes or decisions concerning methods and policies should
rest with him, in view of the lack of experience of the local
people. Nevertheless, every time he takes such matters into his
own hands, he is robbing his brethren in Christ of their rights
and is perhaps unconsciously but very definitely stunting the
growth of that spirit of freedom and progressiveness which is
one of the first essentials to the steady growth of an indigenous
church.

Setting the Standards. The importance of setting and maintaining high standards, both for entrance into full membership
and also for the daily living of the members, has already been
discussed. These standards should be adopted by the church
itself after a careful study of the Scriptures and a prayerful
consideration of the way in which the Scriptural principles can
best be applied to the daily lives and customs of the people
concerned.

In all these matters care must be taken not only that the
right decisions be made and the appropriate actions taken but
that they be made in the appropriate way. The discussions with
the national brethren, necessary in order to enable them to
understand all that is involved, may be long and tiresome, and
often much grace and forbearance will need to be exercised by
the missionary before he is able to carry his point. A successful
missionary will always seek to lead, never to drive, and will be
content to make haste slowly in order that each step taken will

have the unanimous or nearly unanimous approval of all concerned, and that in each decision there may be the definite consciousness that the Great Head of the Church, through the Holy Spirit, is directing in all things.

Transfer of Authority

Anyone who has endeavored to think his way through the main problems involved in the planting of an indigenous church must be deeply impressed with the realization that these are all problems connected with a living organism, rather than a mechanical organization. That being the case, there will be continual calls for adjustments and adaptations to be made so as to fit in with the conditions of any particular field at any particular time. Among these necessary adjustments, foremost in importance will be those connected with the transferring of authority. This will be seen in two distinct relationships.

From Board or Home Committee to Mission. When a new work is inaugurated and a small band of missionaries is sent out for the first time to undertake work in a new mission field, there must be, as has already been indicated, a clear defining and understanding of the responsibilities resting upon both board and mission and the determination of the authority which each possesses. As the mission grows in size and in experience, it is a natural thing to expect that the authority for making certain decisions, respecting personnel, finance, and policies, will be gradually extended by the board to the mission—under proper safeguards.

From Mission to Church. In the previous chapters emphasis has been placed upon the fact that in the planting of an indigenous church one of the very necessary conditions is that from the initial stages responsibility be placed upon the infant church for conducting its own work and that from the very beginning its authority in regard to its own decisions be fully recognized.

There are, however, certain areas of activity where in the nature of the case the mission or the missionaries will have to assume almost entire responsibility and exercise almost sole authority at the beginning, looking forward to a transfer of both to the church as it becomes ready to assume them. These spheres or areas of activity can be classed under the following two categories.

(1) Institutions: There are certain institutions which have proved themselves over and over as being essential to a well-

balanced missionary program. Their nature and development will greatly vary in accordance with the economic conditions and general standards of life in any given mission field. These institutions are those in which are carried on the various phases of medical and educational work.

The medical work includes hospitals, dispensaries, special institutions for lepers, the blind, and the insane. Under the head of educational work will be included all forms of secular education, from kindergartens through elementary and the various forms of secondary and special schools which may be regarded as essential for the development of the work. Medical, industrial, agricultural schools, and schools for the blind have made tremendous contributions to the building up of independent and indigenous churches in many lands. In addition to these, there are the Bible institutes, higher Bible schools, and theological seminaries, which are necessary to the training of the church leadership. When any of these institutions are inaugurated, with the possible exception of primary schools, the missionaries for a time at least must assume full responsibility for their support and management. However, care should be taken from the beginning in all the planning and carrying on of the work, to look forward to the time when the nationals themselves will be in a position to assume the responsibility for the management of those institutions and to take over their financial support as well. Whenever the time is ripe, joint boards of directors should be formed in which Christian nationals and missionaries shall sit together, discussing the problems of management and support; and as the nationals prove their readiness and ability, their representation on the boards and in the official management will also increase, while that of the missionaries will proportionately decrease. No fixed rules can be set as to the time element involved in these matters and while such national representatives can begin early in Bible institutes and primary schools, in the higher and more specialized institutions much longer time will necessarily elapse before conditions will warrant full transfer of authority.

(2) Personnel: In recent years, especially in some mission fields, missions and boards have felt very strongly that the time has already arrived when the local churches should be given a voice in regard to the various problems connected with the best use of the missionary personnel, which is available for work in their territory.

Among the matters on which the advice of the national leaders and churches is being sought and in some cases in which they have a deciding voice are requests for new workers and the assignment of workers to their tasks. This includes the kind of men and women which are most needed and the position which they are to occupy on their arrival. It also includes the decision as to which are the most important needs in order of preference so that the home boards or committees may be guided as to what the strategic needs are, and which they should endeavor to meet first.

It is often a delicate question to decide what disposition should be made, not only of the new workers arriving on the field, but also of the older and more experienced missionaries. Questions of temperament, personality, and equipment often cause acute and distressing situations between missionaries and those among whom they work. An unwillingness to make changes, or a stubborn spirit, may easily cause serious anti-foreign feelings and wreck the usefulness of the missionary involved as well as hinder the progress of the work. When national leaders have developed, as they have in some mission fields, they are being consulted more and more in such matters.

In some foreign mission fields the local churches are being consulted by the missions as to the advisability of the senior missionaries returning at the expiration of their furloughs. Advancing age and weakening health make it difficult to adjust to new conditions—which in some countries are changing with almost kaleidoscopic rapidity. Various methods of adjustment have been worked out for this group of personnel; and the fact that the solutions come with the help of the nationals with whom they have worked is another indication of the way authority and responsibility are being transferred in recent years from the mission to the indigenous church.

QUESTIONS FOR DISCUSSION

1. Discuss the duties and the responsibilities of the board or the home committee.
2. Discuss the duties and the responsibilities of the field mission, in regard to: (a) its members; (b) its budget; and (c) its relation to the national church.
3. Discuss the duties and responsibilities of the national church.
4. Outline changes that should be made in regard to the transfer of authority from the board or the home committee to the mission and from the mission to the national church.

CHAPTER XXIII

THE PRESENT OUTLOOK IN MISSIONS

IT is rather dangerous to attempt to generalize in regard to a world-wide activity such as foreign missions, but it is always helpful to take a bird's eye view of such a majestic undertaking and to examine the general trends and tendencies that characterize the movement.

THE BEGINNING OF A NEW ERA

Students of missions are familiar with the various epochs or eras into which the history of missions has been divided. The most recent of those eras was ushered in by World War II. The great changes in the map of the world brought about by that great conflict are only faint symbols of the far greater changes both in the thinking and in the living conditions of the peoples, both in territories immediately affected by the war and other areas as well. Changed living conditions always result in changed patterns of thought. New ways of thinking in turn bring about new viewpoints and new relationships, both of which vitally affect the methods and policies of foreign mission work. The independence of India with the birth of the two nations of Hindustan and Pakistan, the independence of the Philippines, the breaking down of the colonial administrations of France and Holland in Southeast Asia, the present partition of Korea and the conflict raging there, the spread of Communism in China and its threat to all of Asia, the political changes in Africa due to the changes in the political status of the German and the Italian colonies, and the intense racial antagonisms which have grown up, together with the new economic and industrial conditions—all these are but some of the varied events whose impacts on the thinking and the living conditions of the people affected are as yet more than we have been able fully to appreciate. What will be their effect on the work of foreign missions?

NEW CONDITIONS TO BE FACED

Communism. Communism, with its atheistic propaganda, has infiltrated to some degree every mission field, stirring up

170

the people wherever possible into greater antagonism to the gospel and seeking to inflame them against the missionaries, as those who are the representatives of "Western Imperialism" and other reactionary forces endeavoring to hold back the progress of the Asiatics and the colored races in Africa. Some missions have felt the problem to be so serious that they have appointed certain of their members to make a special study of Communism in order to prepare definite answers to the false claims and criticisms through which many are being deceived. The earnestness and the willingness of the agents of that false ideology to sacrifice everything are a challenge to the missionaries to be ready to give of themselves unsparingly and to be prepared to give sacrificially that the rising tide may be turned back. Only Christ-like humility and patience, consistently and persistently practiced, will be sufficient to give convincing evidence of the falseness of the charges made by Communists and to overcome the poisonous suspicions which their skillful propaganda has already instilled in people's thinking. The witness of a Christ-like life amidst all the pressure and strains which are part of a normal missionary life will be the most effective repudiation of the charges which are commonly made by the protagonists of that Satanic system. It has already made astounding headway in the Far East and has become by far the most serious challenge to the Christian faith.

Acute Economic Pressure. With the devaluation of currencies in many lands and the almost astronomic inflation, economic pressure has greatly increased and the struggle for existence has become acute. It is in almost every case unwise, if not impossible, for the missionary to attempt to live on the same scale as those among whom he is working, even though he is seeking to present the Lord Jesus Christ. The gap therefore in the economic standards of living, unless great care is taken, may become a serious barrier. Unless he is prepared to be at all times open and sympathetic in his readiness to listen to their problems, a spirit of jealousy or covetousness may easily grow up among the nationals or a feeling that since he, the foreign missionary, is living on another level he cannot understand the difficulties in their lives.

Nationalism. One of the outstanding results of the changes mentioned in the earlier part of this chapter has been the tremendous upsurge of national and racial consciousness which has taken place all over the world and especially among those people whom we have habitually thought of as oppressed and backward. They react bitterly to what they think are character-istics of imperialistic policies and they have become peculiarly sensitive to anything which even resembles a patronizing attitude on the part of missionaries. This in turn has brought about a new spirit of independent thought and action in the national churches. For the most part this is a healthy thing, but it has meant that the foreign missionary can no longer think of himself as indispensable in any given position and he must be prepared to counsel and advise, but not to command. He will need increasingly to exert great caution not to give offense or injure feelings by exhibiting attitudes or making statements, that might be interpreted as betraying a superiority complex or a spirit of condescension. Along with this condition in many mission fields there is a far greater readiness on the part of the nationals and their Christian leaders to criticize the foreign missionary and not to receive him fully into their confidence, unless or until he has proved himself to their satisfaction.

New Problems. Another complicating factor in missionary work today is caused by the rapid and radical changes in the social structures in many lands. In the Orient especially, where ancestor worship and the authority of the family and clan have held sway for centuries but have been largely swept away during the past decade, a revolution has taken place in individual rela-tionships and thinking which is almost impossible for people in this country to realize. Similarly, the tremendous social and economic changes which have taken place in Japan since World War II have brought about equally great changes in the thinking of that vigorous and active people. In Africa, especially South Africa, sweeping changes have come about through the vast industrial developments; and inter-racial problems in which African, Indian, and white races are all involved have arisen to a very acute degree. The unrest and uncertainty with regard to political changes and the problems of inflation and exchange due to the rapidly changing economic conditions, all are increasingly forcing the missions to think seriously through many of their policies. These conditions in themselves are making many people realize the absolute necessity to see that the national churches, already formed, become indigenous just as rapidly as possible and that all new work to be opened will be planned with this in view from the very inception.

New Forms of Activity

With new conditions all over the world, as might be expected, various new forms of Christian activity which have become prominent in the home lands are now being made use of to good effect on the mission fields. Impressive *revival movements* are taking place in many lands. The great work of the Spirit of God in Ethiopia has already been referred to in previous chapters, but reports of similar workings of the Spirit are being received from other lands also. In addition to these, evangelistic campaigns are being planned and carried out in many places with a view to producing a new impact upon the people and awakening them to the fact that the Gospel is a virile and vital force which cannot remain passive in the lives of those who know and love the Lord Jesus Christ, but which impels them into dynamic action for the sake of their fellow-men who have no knowledge of the Saviour. These campaigns are usually effective to the degree in which they bring into action the rank and file of the Christians in the area; for the presence and power of the Lord Jesus Christ is always more clearly seen in the changed lives of fellow nationals than in those of foreigners. Today all such movements should as far as possible be directed and carried out by nationals, who are in a far better position to understand the psychology of the best method of approach to their fellow countrymen.

Youth Movement. These are being utilized to a good advantage in many places. Inter-Varsity Christian Fellowship, Youth for Christ International, Young Life Campaign, and Child Evangelism Fellowship, all of which have made a great place for themselves in the Christian movement in America, are now branching out to some foreign mission fields and are proving themselves valuable allies to the work of foreign missions in those areas. All of these movements which do so much to capture the imagination and the interest of young people and children, are of very great importance as arms of the church. In many places missions are lending some of their members to these movements in order to bring about the closest co-operation possible and to insure that all of the young people reached may be guided into the proper churches, where their future training and nurture in the Christian faith will be maintained.

Broadcasting. This is another activity which has sprung up recently in mission circles and is proving its great value wherever it has been used. The great missionary broadcasting stations in Ecuador (HCJB) and in Manila (DZAZ) and in Africa (ELWA) are already reaching many countries in both hemispheres with the gospel in the native tongues. This has resulted in the establishment of many new churches. Similar stations in Hongkong and Central America are proving of immense value in reaching out into many homes, which would otherwise be untouched and are almost unreachable by the gospel. The broadcasting of the gospel in this way has already been clearly demonstrated to be a strong means of counteracting the insidious Communist propaganda being carried on in those lands.

Needs for the Future

In view of these new conditions as noted and with the use of the new activities above mentioned, what are the specific needs and what is the prospect for missions in the near future?

It would seem unnecessary to say that the uncertainty and the difficulties facing the foreign missionary everywhere in themselves constitute a tremendous challenge to the whole church in the homelands to bestir herself in a new way to prayer and to sacrificial giving on behalf of the cause of world-wide evangelization, that once again it may be proved that "Man's extremity is God's opportunity."

With so many doors already closed and the prospects of others closing within the next five or ten years, there should be a spirit of urgency, of great urgency, in all our missionary thinking and planning. This spirit of urgency should lead all those in missionary circles to think anew along several lines. Some of these are here given.

Revaluation of Mission Policies and Methods. Nearly all business organizations, especially those of international scope, are carefully revaluating their policies, and in the light of new conditions are ruthlessly scrapping old policies and methods in favor of others which they consider better suited to the new day. Missions should be prepared to face the same problems with equal determination and readiness to change policies which, while they may have been effective in the past, are no longer geared to the needs and to the pace of the new age which is upon us. This will require a spirit of humble self-examination and a conscientious endeavor on the part of all to take an objective view and as far as possible to remove all thoughts of bias or prestige which would in any way color their thinking.

Chapter XXIV

THE MISSIONARY FOR THE NEW DAY

A S we have already seen, the era of missions into which we are now entering will be very different from all that have gone before. New conditions, new attitudes among the peoples in the various mission fields, requiring new techniques by missions and missionaries—all will require careful and prayerful consideration and planning. What then will be the qualifications for missionaries that will best enable them to become useful instruments in the hands of the Lord in winning people to faith in Him, in developing national Christian leaders, and in establishing virile indigenous churches?

These delicate and complex conditions already mentioned and the pressing urgency for the work to be done now present a tremendous challenge to any true servant of God who has the necessary physical health and mental ability and freeness to go.

Adaptability. One of the first essentials to being a successful missionary has always been a readiness and an ability to adapt to new conditions. The need for such today is greater then ever before. With the continuous and rapid changes taking place all over the world, life must necessarily become a series of adjustments to meet them. This requires the continued use of what has been called "sanctified imagination," in order that the individual missionary may be enabled by the Spirit of God to see himself through the eyes of those among whom he is living, and then so to conduct himself that in all things he may be "void of offense," and may continually exhibit the grace and winsomeness of the Lord Jesus Christ.

This adaptability is vitally needed in his relationships with the nationals, both Christian and non-Christian; it is equally needed in his relationships with fellow missionaries. Personnel problems among the missionaries are the most difficult to solve and are far-reaching in their effects upon the work and life of the church. It is tragically easy for those living in small mission stations, far removed from any other white or Anglo-Saxon neighbors, to develop sources of irritation and friction which destroy all sense of true fellowship in the Lord and bring defeat and shame to all concerned. In such cases, mere adaptability is not sufficient. It requires God-given grace and Spirit-led co-operation to bring about and to maintain harmony and love so that the work of the Lord may progress to His honor and glory.

As part of this adaptability, there needs to be a holy boldness under the direction of the Holy Spirit to step out in faith in an effort to meet new conditions with new methods. The danger of "getting into ruts" is as great abroad as it is at home and these "ruts" apply not only to ways of working but equally to attitudes, and habits of thought. Freshness of mind and a spirit of expectancy because God has promised and will keep His Word are valuable assets in meeting the baffling problems of foreign heathendom with what often seems "so little and so few."

Humility. A few years ago while attending a panel discussion a foreign missions conference, I heard the qualifications of a foreign missionary being discussed. Toward the end of the period a missionary with years of experience said that in his opinion the first and foremost qualification was humility; the second qualification was humility; and the third qualification also was humility! That is always true. In the Orient as elsewhere humility is regarded as a mark of a great man.

Habitual humility is careful and continually alert not to say or do things which might unnecessarily injure feelings. There must also be a readiness to offer an apology whenever offense has been taken, even though there seems no rational cause for the injured feelings. In Oriental countries where formal and elaborate salutations are still customary, every new missionary should make a point of learning and observing them carefully. For example, it was years before I learned that it was considered very impolite for a younger man to keep his glasses on while saluting an older one, or that to stand on the steps of a home and greet a guest who was standing on a lower level was equally bad form. Had national self-consciousness or super-sensitiveness been as acute in my earlier missionary experience as it became later, I tremble to think of what unfortunate impressions I might have unwittingly created! In conversation with some Korean Christian friends on one occasion one of them told me that he was prejudiced for years against the gospel because the first missionary he ever saw had failed to remove his shoes before entering their house and was sitting on the floor with his shoes on, unconsciously outraging the feelings of his companions, to say nothing of soiling the matting on which others in their white robes would soon have to sit. A humble alertness might have avoided this offense and won a soul.

It requires the grace of humility for a missionary to push forward his national fellow workers and urge them to accept the positions of authority and honor in the church, when he knows that he himself could doubtless do the job more effectively. Since it is their church, however, they are the ones to direct it as soon as they are able, while the humble missionary steps back and busies himself with other tasks. This is all part, however, of being an ambassador for the Lord Jesus Christ.

Complete Consecration to the Will of God. Another essential qualification for fruitful work is the unshakable conviction that the missionary has been called by God and definitely led by Him to his particular field and work. Only· thus can the hardships and loneliness, the discouragements and misunderstandings be accepted as God's appointments, and met and conquered with that quiet confidence which comes only to those who are day by day conscious of the guiding and enabling power of the Holy Spirit.

Because of the strangeness and often startling differences in the thinking and customs of the nationals, every missionary, in whatever foreign field, will have to face situations of which he had never dreamed, and these can be successfully met only under the direct guidance of the Holy Spirit. Problems involving the heathen practices of concubinage, ancestor worship, marriage and burial customs, and the place of woman are often extremely intricate, and special wisdom is required to make the right decisions and set the right standards. Obedience to the Spirit's leading is a "must" in such situations.

Love for the People. A sincere love for the nationals is another requisite, absolutely essential to successful work. Without it, winning their confidence and respect is simply impossible in these days of international suspicion. Such love is not natural, and many a new missionary has gravely questioned the possibility of ever overcoming the barriers of dirt, poverty, smells, and customs so repugnant to him. However, in a short time the consciousness that it is the love of God that has called him to the task breaks through the barriers and a deep-seated affection arises, especially for those who are his brethren in Christ.

This love will manifest itself in various ways. It brings

with it an earnest desire and a determination to leave no stone unturned in learning the language and in becoming familiar with the social customs of the people as soon as possible. Many a missionary's usefulness has been greatly handicapped by his willingness to get along with a limited vocabulary and imperfect pronunciation. Others have unwittingly made wrong impressions on many whom they desired to win for Christ by remaining ignorant of matters of etiquette and social usage.

This love of the Lord is needed to make a missionary slow to take offense in the face of deliberate insults by anti-foreign non-Christians or even criticisms from his Christian brethren. A readiness to forgive will always be a mark of a true ambassador of the Lord Jesus Christ and will be used by the Holy Spirit to make deep impressions on the lives of these new associates; it may be a leading factor in eventually winning them to the Lord.

It requires real love to exercise the needed patience and forbearance in counseling with the nationals in regard to their problems. A prominent national church leader in an Oriental country said not long ago there was a fear that the younger new men coming to the mission field were not taking sufficient time to listen to their views sympathetically and to pray with them with open minds until they could come together in their opinions. Consecrated love and waiting on the Lord will bring the needed patience for such situations.

Real love of God as manifested in a consistent attitude of Christian courtesy and thoughtfulness for the feelings of others is also the best safe-guard against the anti-foreign complex mentioned in previous paragraphs. It always eventually works.

A Robust Spiritual Life. For a successful missionary career a robust and vigorous spiritual life is absolutely necessary. To this end, the missionary must take time for daily Bible study and personal devotions. The depressing effect of living in the midst of foreign heathenism is something which must be experienced to be understood. The constant daily pressure upon every missionary, regardless of his particular assignment of work, and the resultant drain upon his spiritual resources demand a continual refilling of spiritual power. Most missionaries live in small and often isolated mission stations where there are no contacts with the outside world, few if any opportunities to attend Bible conferences, and almost no other human being to whom to go for comfort, encouragement, and counsel. There is a continual draining out to needy souls, answering their questions, discussing with them their problems, seeking to win them to the Lord, and then to lead them on to life on a higher plane. Therefore a missionary must know the secret of tapping the resources of power and refreshment for himself and of receiving the guidance of the Holy Spirit. He must use these resources for himself in order to be a winsome witness to the gospel of the altogether lovely Lord Jesus.

QUESTIONS FOR DISCUSSION

1. Make a list in order of preference of what you consider are the necessary qualifications for a successful missionary.
2. Are there any fundamental differences between the qualifications for successful foreign missionaries and for pastors in the homeland? If so, what are they?
3. What do you consider are the ways whereby in these days of nationalistic consciousness the foreign missionary can most effectively guard against causing offense and thereby raising problems?
4. Discuss the proper attitude of the missionary to the religions of the people among whom he is working. Should he publicly criticize and point out their fallacies?
5. Discuss some of the problems involved in the relation of the missionary to the government officials and what should be his attitude toward them?

INDEX

SCRIPTURE QUOTATIONS